T0024625

THE EVERYTHING® KIDS' Math Puzzles for Kindergarten

Learn about Counting, Measuring, Adding, and More with 100 Fun Puzzles!

Hannah Whately

ADAMS MEDIA
NEW YORK LONDON TORONTO SYDNEY NEW DELHI

Adams Media
An Imprint of Simon & Schuster, Inc.
100 Technology Center Drive
Stoughton, Massachusetts 02072

Copyright © 2021 by Simon & Schuster, Inc.

All rights reserved, including the right to reproduce this book or portions thereof in any form whatsoever. For information address Adams Media Subsidiary Rights Department, 1230 Avenue of the Americas, New York, NY 10020.

An Everything® Series Book.
Everything® and everything.com® are registered trademarks of Simon & Schuster, Inc.

First Adams Media trade paperback edition July 2021

ADAMS MEDIA and colophon are trademarks of Simon & Schuster.

For information about special discounts for bulk purchases, please contact Simon & Schuster Special Sales at 1-866-506-1949 or business@simonandschuster.com.

The Simon & Schuster Speakers Bureau can bring authors to your live event. For more information or to book an event contact the Simon & Schuster Speakers Bureau at 1-866-248-3049 or visit our website at www.simonspeakers.com.

Interior design by Erin Alexander
Illustrations by Jim Steck

Manufactured in the United States of America

Printed by LSC Communications, Crawfordsville, IN, U.S.A.

2 2022

ISBN 978-1-5072-1614-9

Many of the designations used by manufacturers and sellers to distinguish their products are claimed as trademarks. Where those designations appear in this book and Simon & Schuster, Inc., was aware of a trademark claim, the designations have been printed with initial capital letters.

Contents

Introduction. 5

Chapter 1
Numbers and Counting (Numbers Up to 10) · 7

Ice Cream 8
Under the Sea 9
Goldfish Bowls 10
Space Aliens 11
Counting Raindrops 12
School Buses 13
Birthday Cake 14
Ladybugs 15
Countdown 16
Bubbles of 10 17
Find the Fish 18
Scarves 19
Number Squares (Numbers to 10) 20

Chapter 2
Numbers and Counting (11-20) · 21

On the Farm 22
Balloons 23
Wide Awake. 24
Bouncy Balls 25
Puzzle Pieces 26
Which Cheetah? 27
Jack and the Beanstalk 28
Spider Maze. 29
Cupcakes 30
At the Fairground 31
Rainbow Snail. 32
Flowerpots 33
Number Squares (11–20) 34

Chapter 3
Comparing Numbers · 35

Sandcastles 36
Peapods 37
Butterflies. 38
Watermelon Seeds 39
Which Dog?. 40
Dinosaurs 41
Number Pies 42
Crocodiles. 43
Pizzas 44
Marbles 45
Storming the Castle 46
Apples 47

Chapter 4
Counting to 100 · 49

Houses. 50
Polly 51
Trains 52
Caterpillars 53
Bird's Nest 54
What's My Name? 55
Up in the Sky 56
Paint Splatters 57
Who's Swimming? 58
Counting Crayons 59
Party Penguins 60
Jumping Frog 61

Chapter 5
Adding · 63

Ducklings 64
Which Carrot? 65
Sunflower 66
Let's Play! 67
Library Books 68
In the Rainforest 69
Dice 70
Hamburgers 71
Strawberry Picking 72
Twins 73
Hot-Air Balloons 74

Chapter 6
Subtracting · 75

Fruit Salad 76
At the Bakery 77
Hats 78
Squirrels 79
Bears and Honey 80
Bees 81
Fishing 82
On the Beach 83
Flying Saucers 84
Happy or Sad? 85

Chapter 7
Measurement and Data · 87

Which Animal? 88
Sorting Socks 89
Legs 90
Snowmen 91
In the Backyard 92
Pairs 93
Gifts 94
On the Move 95
Pencil Case 96
Enchanted Forest 97
Water 98
How's the Weather? 99
Jelly Beans 100

Chapter 8
Shapes and Patterns · 101

Everyday Shapes 102
Mice and Cheese 103
Jewels 104
Design a Hat 105
Kites 106
Robot 107
Cookies 108
Shape Pictures 109
Flat or Solid? 110
Shape People 111
Traffic Light 112
Shapes All Around 113
Toy Store 114
What Am I? 115
Cone or Cylinder? 116
What Is Missing? 117

Answers 119

Introduction

Kindergarten-aged children are eager to learn, and math activities during these early years should be fun and engaging. Although they will learn a lot about math with their class, there are many activities that can be done at home to reinforce these all-important skills. Encourage your child to count apples in a bowl, name the shapes of blocks and other toys, and identify patterns all around them. Or take the time to sit together and try some of the colorful, fun, and educational puzzles in *The Everything® Kids' Math Puzzles for Kindergarten*.

This collection of 100 puzzles provides an enjoyable way for your child to practice and develop important early math skills. These puzzles make math fun by using colorful and appealing themes to capture a young child's interest. The book is divided into eight chapters, each focusing on a math topic that corresponds to the US Common Core State Standards. Your child will practice counting, comparing numbers, addition, and subtraction. Later puzzles introduce the concepts of measurement and data, shapes, position, patterns, and position words.

All your child needs are a pencil and some crayons, markers, or colored pencils. And you, of course, to read instructions out loud and encourage your child as they complete the puzzles. Your child will give answers in lots of different ways—by writing a number in a box; drawing a line to the correct answer; or coloring, circling, or putting a checkmark next to an object. They'll be practicing fine motor skills in addition to math.

Each chapter focuses on a different math topic and set of skills. While the puzzles can be done in any order, it's a good idea to move through the ones in Chapters 1 through 6 from beginning to end, because they increase a bit in difficulty. Mix in puzzles from the last two chapters for variety. Here are the things your child will be learning as you work together on the puzzles and activities:

- **Numbers and counting.** These puzzles focus on recognizing and naming numbers and developing counting skills. Your child will solve puzzles by ordering and writing numbers all the way up to 20.
- **Comparing numbers.** In these puzzles your child will look at the numbers to 10 *in relation to each other*. They will compare groups of objects to see which has more, fewer, or the same. They will also compare written numerals.
- **Counting to 100.** In kindergarten, children learn to count all the way up to 100. Fun activities like connect the dots, number mazes, and hundreds charts help them practice ordering all those numbers. You'll also find puzzles that feature skip counting by 10.
- **Adding and subtracting within 10.** Some easier puzzles involve adding and subtracting with the help of pictures, while others involve simple written number sentences or word problems.
- **Measurement and data.** In these puzzles, your child will be looking at different measurable attributes such as length, weight, and capacity. Some puzzles ask your child to sort objects according to their type or properties.
- **Shape, position, and patterns.** In kindergarten, children are introduced to both two-dimensional and three-dimensional shapes. Easy shape puzzles ask your child to identify and name shapes, and more challenging ones direct them to sort shapes according to their attributes. Other puzzles feature shape and color patterns, as well as position words such as *above*, *beside*, and *in front of*.

Don't expect to do too many puzzles in one sitting—a handful of puzzles at a time is best at this age. To help your child get the most out of these puzzles, work through them together. Read the instructions aloud and talk about the math on the page. Encourage your child to use the pictures to help them as they do the puzzles. It may be useful to have something you can count with (such as counters or building blocks) on hand, particularly for the addition and subtraction chapters.

If you come across a puzzle that seems too challenging for your child, that's okay. Leave it and come back to it at another time. At this age, children are developing in leaps and bounds, so a puzzle they may find tricky now will probably seem like a piece of cake later in the kindergarten year. The most important thing is that you and your child have fun working through the book—counting people at the fairground, following a spider maze, or sorting socks. I do hope your child has fun with these puzzles (and learns a bit of math along the way too!).

Chapter 1

Numbers and Counting (Numbers Up to 10)

As you probably already know, young children love counting. In this chapter, there are lots of opportunities to put those counting skills into practice. Your child will count groups of up to 10 objects and order numbers both forward and backward. To help with building number sense, numbers are shown in lots of different ways—in the form of a group of objects, as circles in a ten frame, as tally marks, as dots on dice, or as a written word. It's a lot to learn, but finding underwater creatures, celebrating a birthday, and helping to launch a rocket make it entertaining as well as instructive.

Ice Cream

It's time for ice cream!
Count the dots on the dice, and then use the code to color the picture.

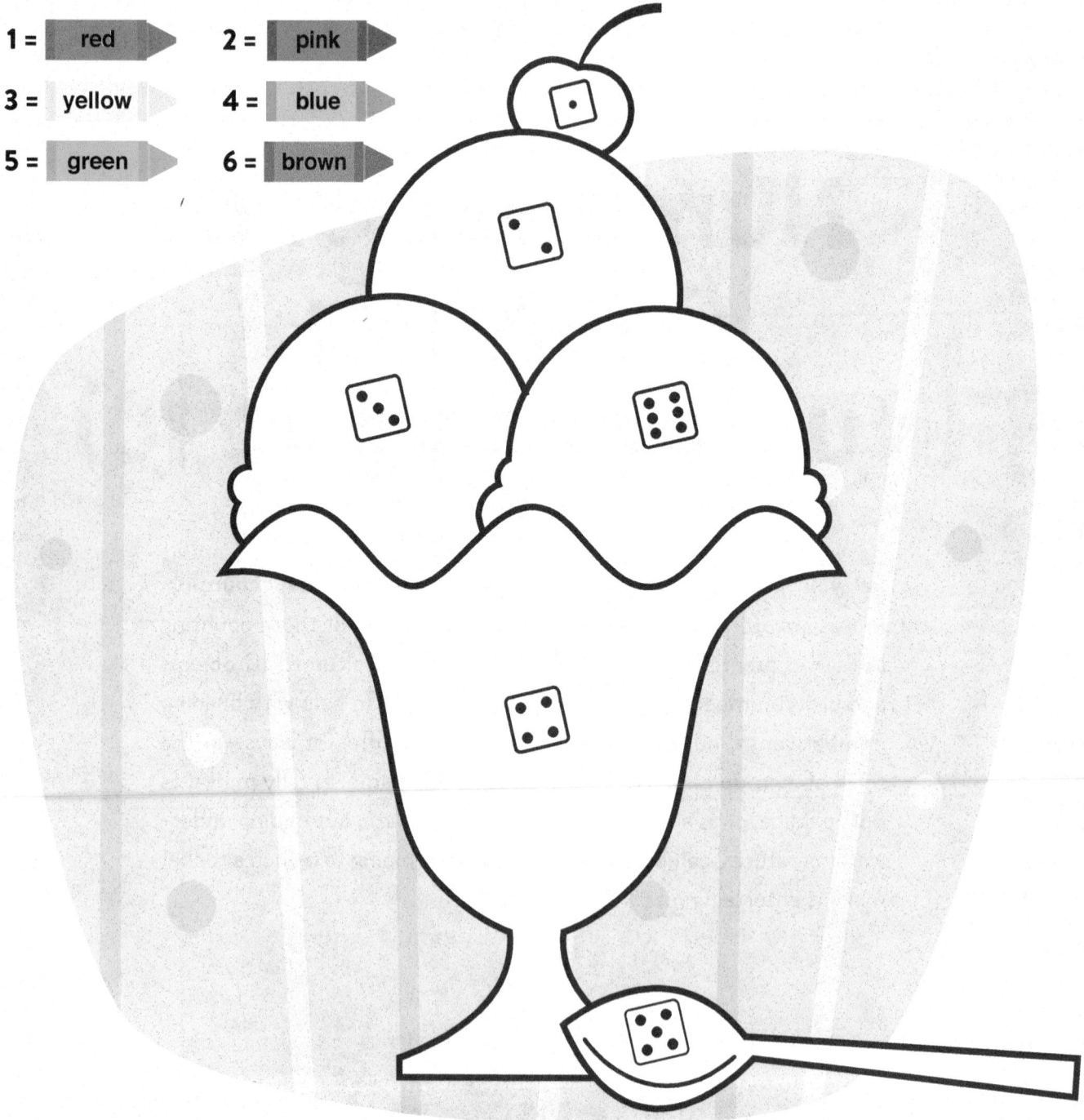

Under the Sea

Can you count the different sea creatures in the picture?
For each type of sea creature, write the number you counted in the box.

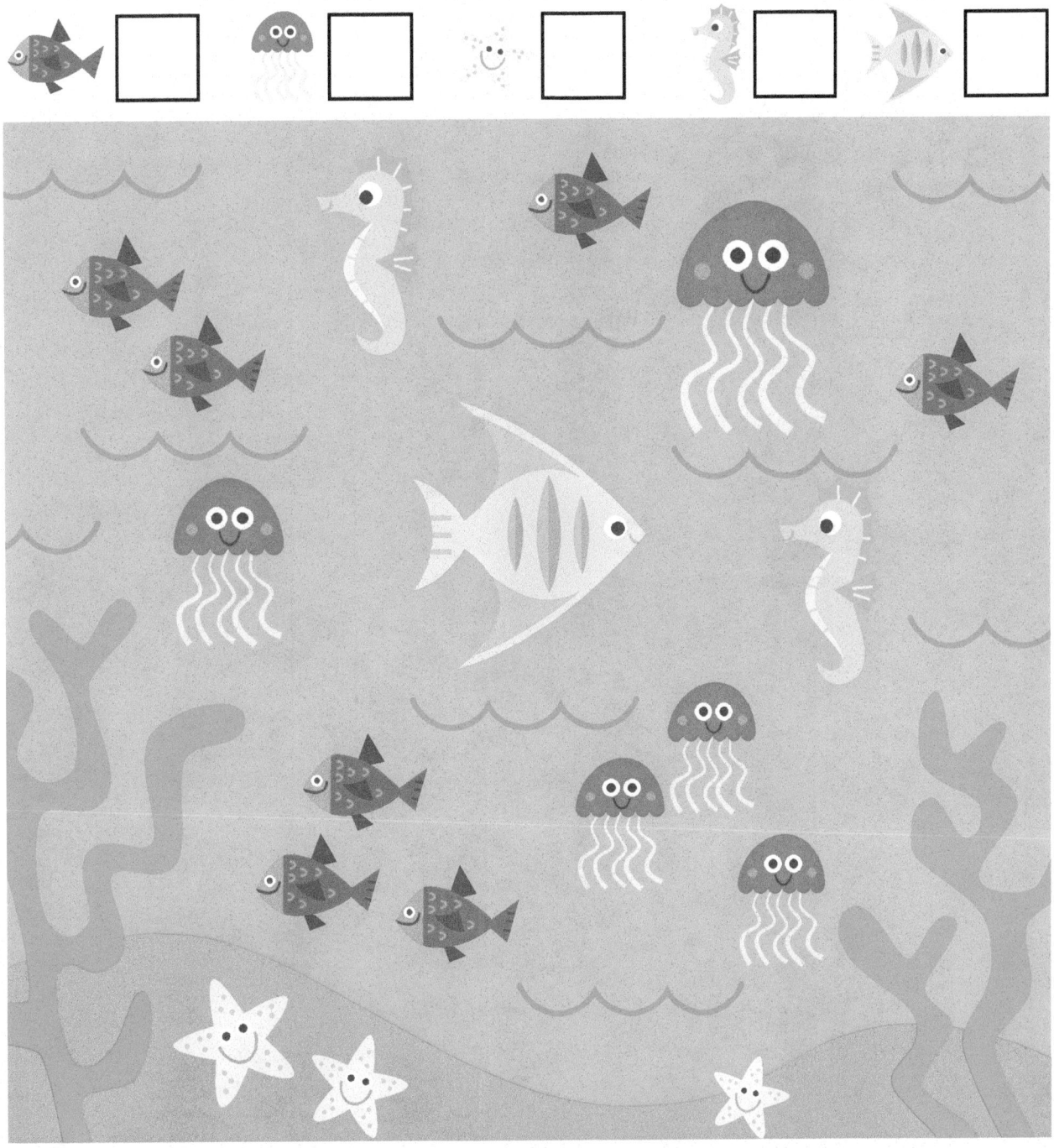

Goldfish Bowls

Put a checkmark (✓) next to the bowls that have **2** fish and **4** bubbles.

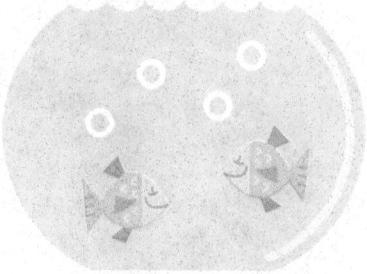

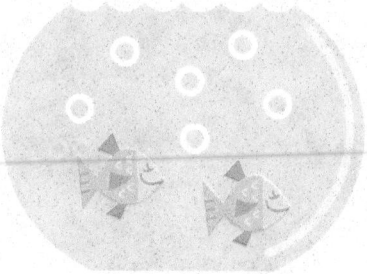

Space Aliens

Here is a space alien from a faraway planet.
Count its eyes, arms, and legs, and then fill in the boxes.

It has ☐ eyes.

It has ☐ arms.

It has ☐ legs.

Can you draw your own space alien in the box? Give your alien **5** eyes, **2** arms, and **3** legs.

Counting Raindrops

Can you count the raindrops under each cloud? Draw a line to the matching umbrella.

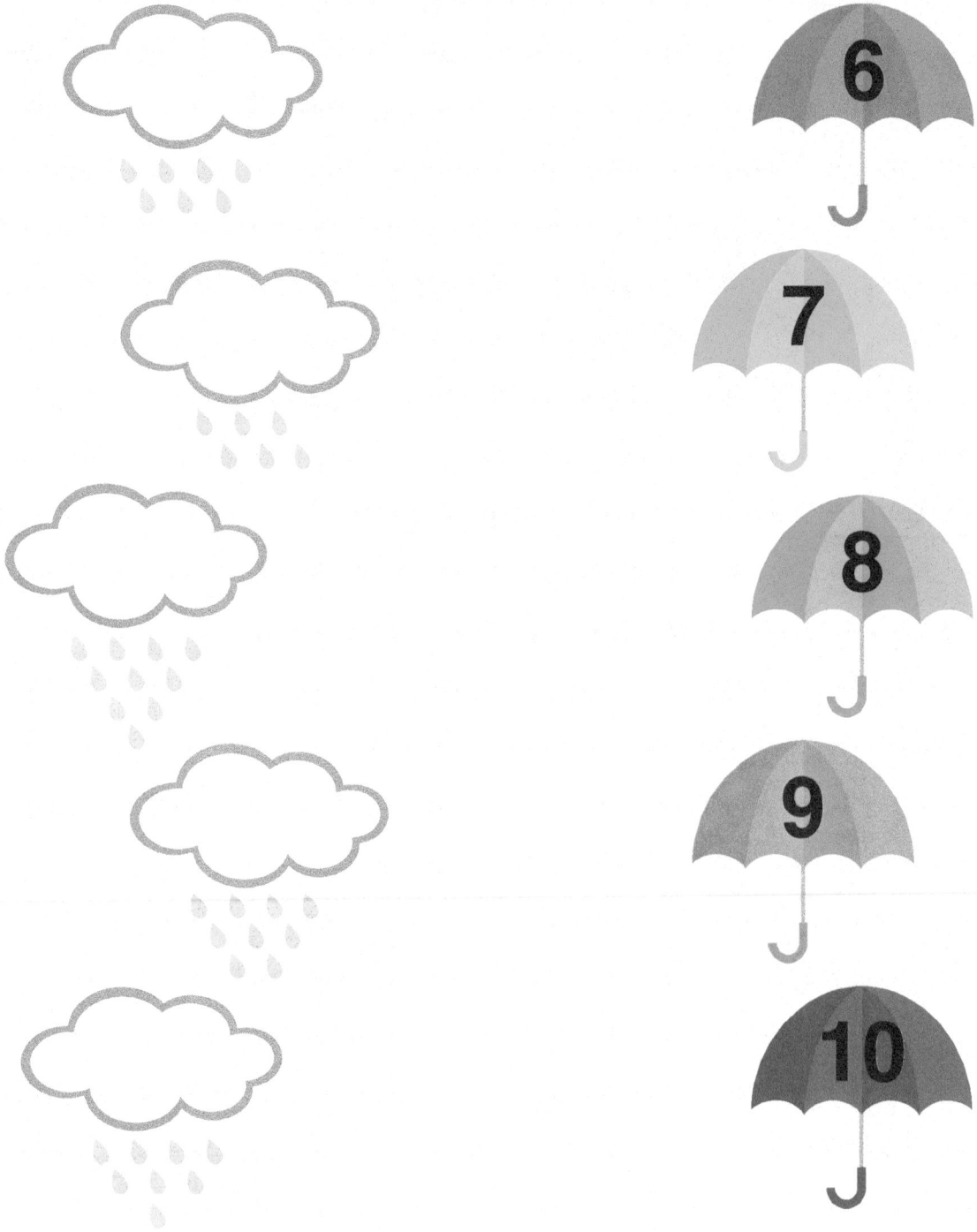

School Buses

Can you count the smiley faces in each school bus?
Write the number you counted in the box.

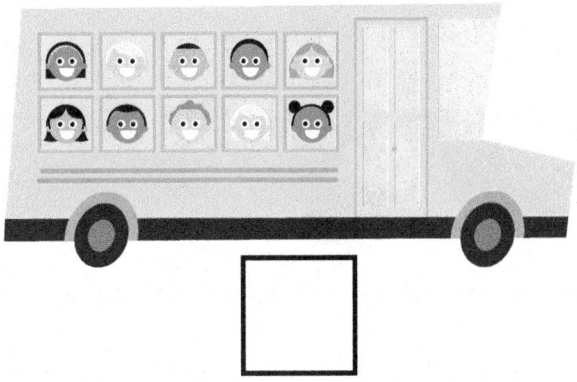

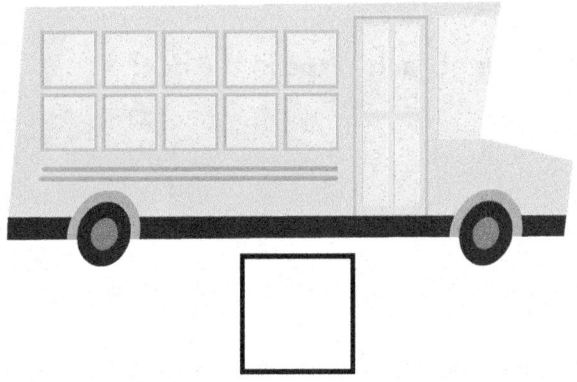

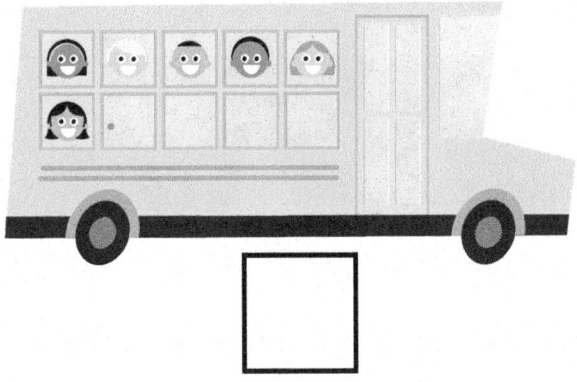

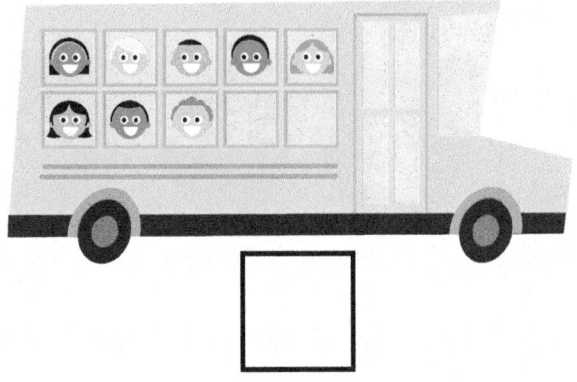

Draw **5** smiley faces in this bus and color the picture.

Birthday Cake

It's my birthday. I am **6** today!

Can you count the different shapes on the cake and write the number of each shape in the box?

There are ☐  shapes.

There are ☐  shapes.

There are ☐  shapes.

Draw more candles on the cake so that it has **6** altogether.

Ladybugs

Look at the ladybugs on this leaf.

Can you circle the ladybug that does **not** have **7** spots?

Add more spots to this ladybug so it has **7** spots too.

Countdown

Can you help count down from **10** to **1** to launch the rocket?
Fill in the missing numbers.

Bubbles of 10

Look at the numbers shown in the bubbles.

Color all the bubbles that show **10**.

How many bubbles did you color?

Find the Fish

Can you help the cat get to the fish?
Find the path through the maze that follows the numbers **1** to **10** in order.

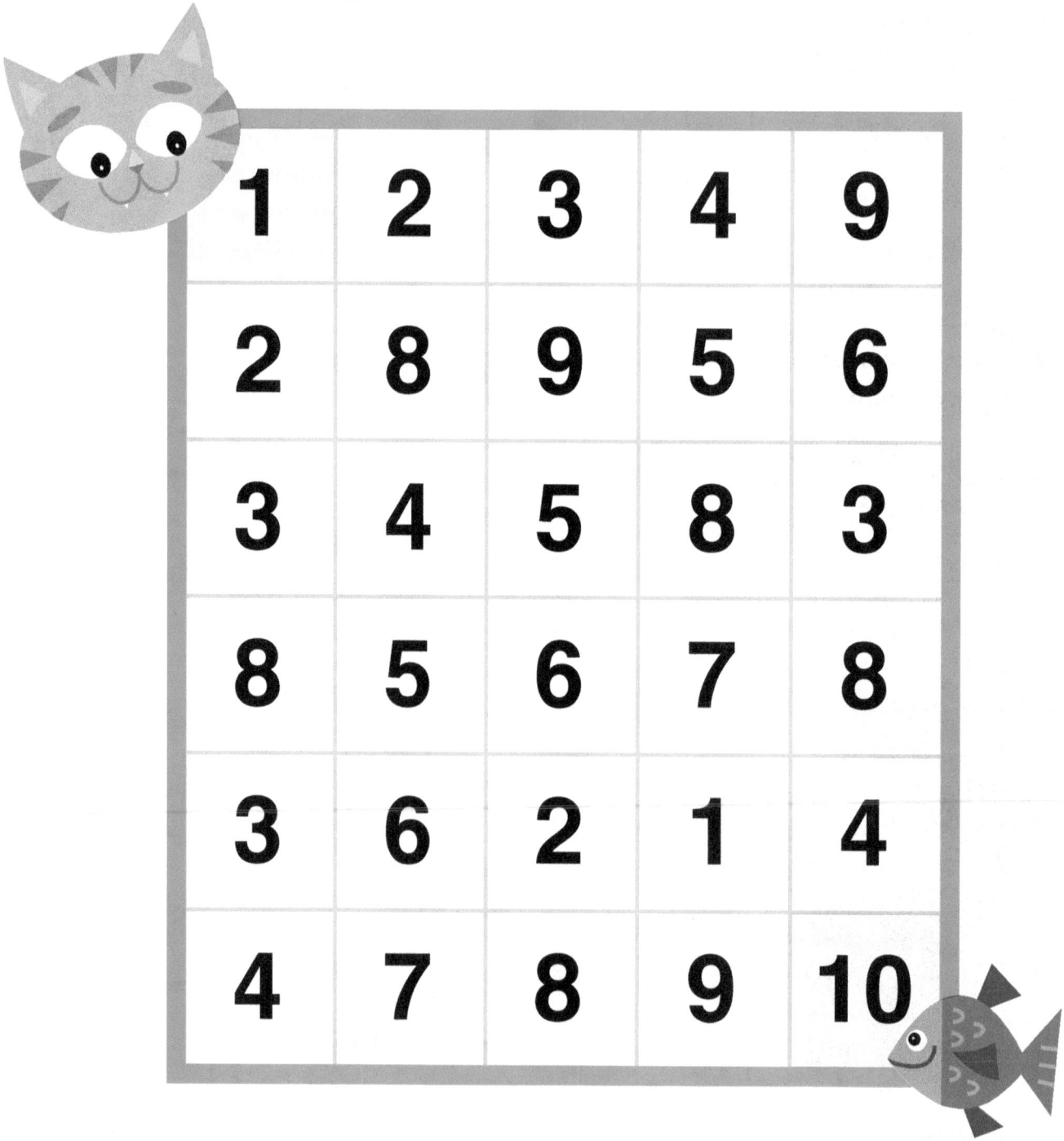

1	2	3	4	9
2	8	9	5	6
3	4	5	8	3
8	5	6	7	8
3	6	2	1	4
4	7	8	9	10

Scarves

Can you write the missing numbers on these colorful scarves?

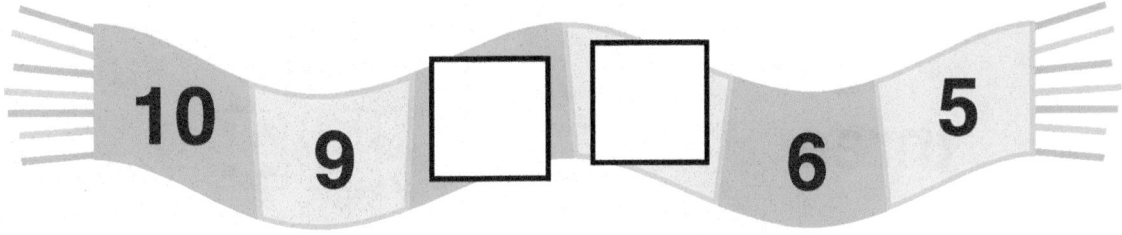

Number Squares (Numbers to 10)

Each row shows four different numbers.
Put a checkmark (✓) under the number you are looking for.

Which square shows **7**?

8

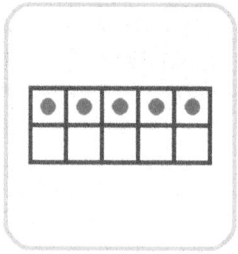

six

Which square shows **3**?

zero

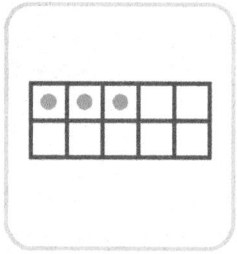

Which square shows **10**?

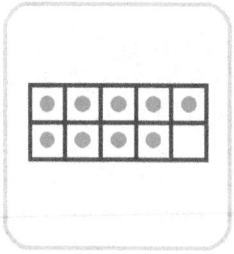

Which square shows **5**?

three

4

Chapter 2

Numbers and Counting (11-20)

The numbers 11–20 can be tricky to learn. In addition to learning the names of these numbers, your child is also beginning to write numbers that have two digits. As in the 1–10 puzzles, numbers 11 to 20 are shown in a variety of ways—as a group of objects, as a written numeral, or as dots or tally marks. Some of the later puzzles in this chapter incorporate base 10 blocks, which help children to see numbers broken down into 10s and 1s. This collection of puzzles, including connect the dots, mazes, and coded coloring pictures, will help your child continue their counting journey past 10.

On the Farm

Use the code to color the farmyard picture.

11 = green	12 = brown	13 = yellow
14 = blue	15 = pink	16 = red

Balloons

Use red to color all the balloons that show the number **18.**

Color the rest of the balloons using your favorite colors.

Wide Awake

It's nighttime and somebody is wide awake. Starting with **11**, connect the dots in order from **11** to **20** to finish the picture. Then color it in.

How many stars can you count in the night sky?

Bouncy Balls

Bouncy balls are bouncing everywhere! Can you help the girls catch and sort the bouncy balls? Draw a line to match each ball to the correct basket.

16

13

18

17

20

19

12

14

11

15

Puzzle Pieces

These puzzle pieces are all mixed up!
Count the shapes in each piece, and then draw a line to the correct number.

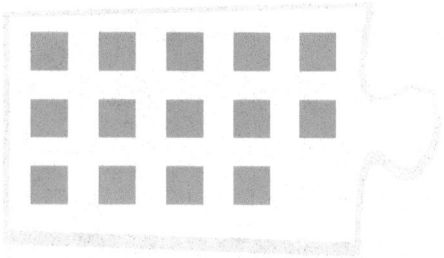

18

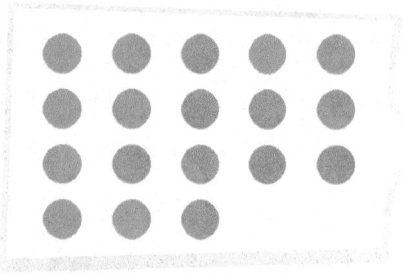

20

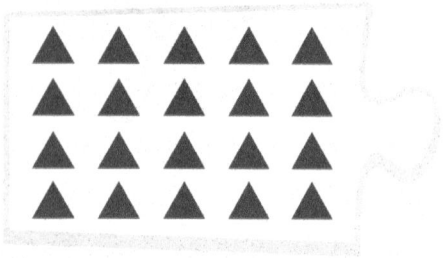

13

14

17

Which Cheetah?

One of these cheetahs has **12** spots on it. Which one?
When you find it, color it in.

Jack and the Beanstalk

Spider Maze

Can you find your way through the maze to the spider in the middle?
Follow the numbers in order to get to **20**.

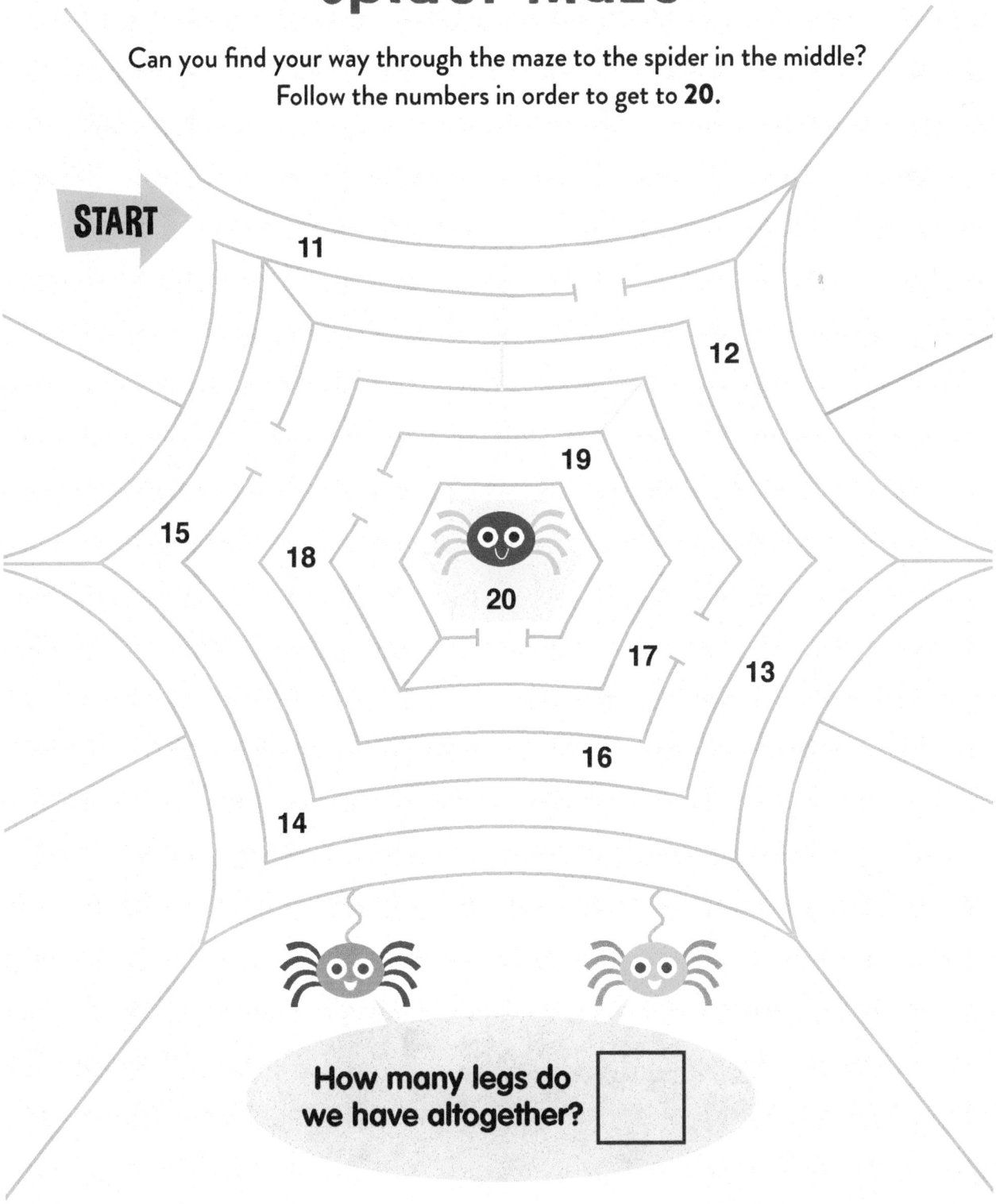

Cupcakes

Look at the cupcakes on each tray. Can you fill in the missing numbers?

At the Fairground

Count the people in different parts of the fairground.
Then write the numbers in the boxes.

How many people are on the Ferris wheel?

How many people are on the roller coaster?

How many people are on the train?

How many people are waiting for a hot dog?

Rainbow Snail

There are some numbers missing from the snail's shell. Can you fill them in?

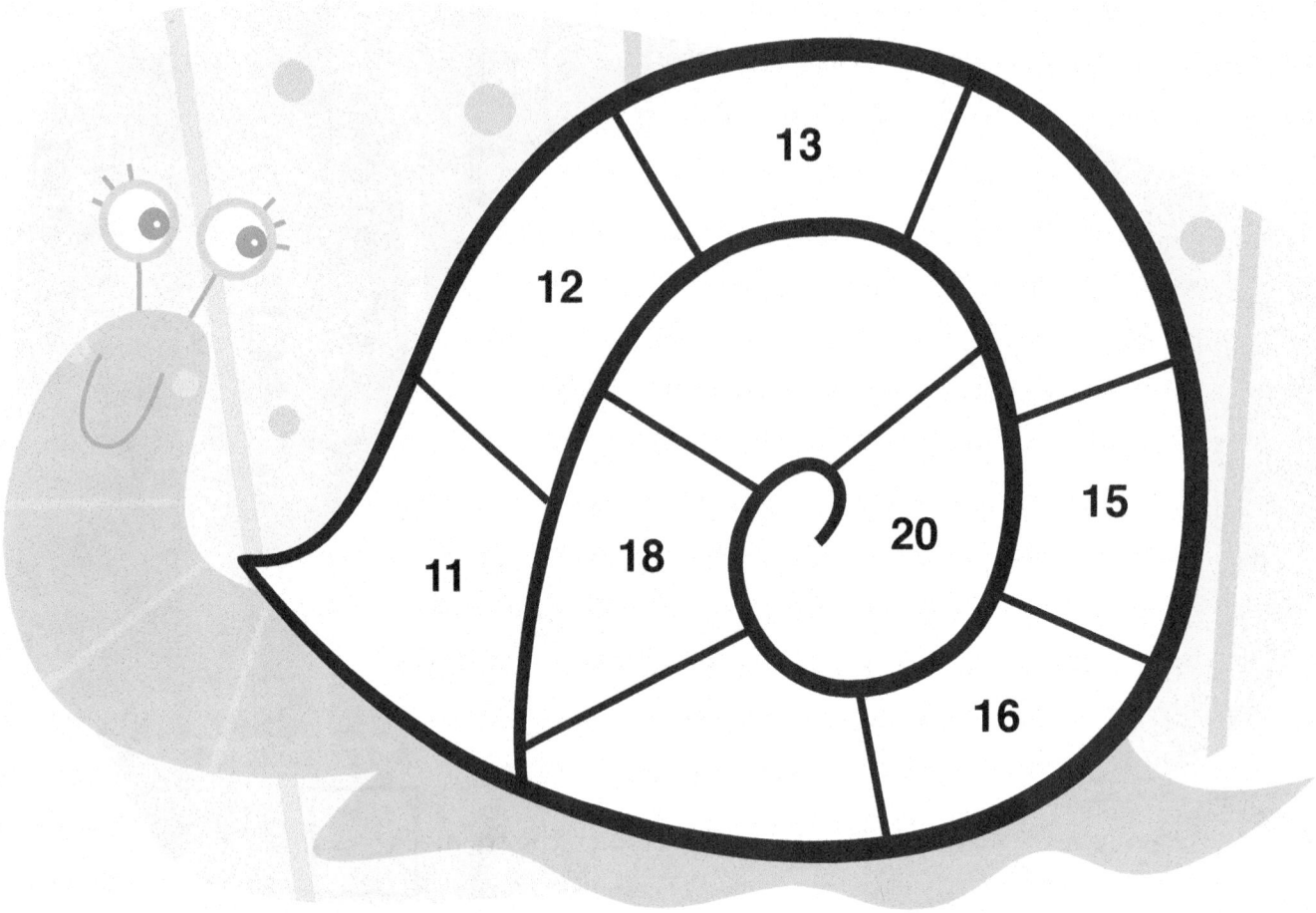

The snail's shell needs some color. Color it using the code.

11 and **12** = blue **13** and **14** = green **15** and **16** = yellow

17 and **18** = orange **19** and **20** = red

Flowerpots

Count the blocks on each flowerpot.
Then color the flower with the matching number.

Number Squares (11-20)

Each row shows four different numbers.
Put a checkmark (✓) under the number you are looking for.

Which square shows **16**?

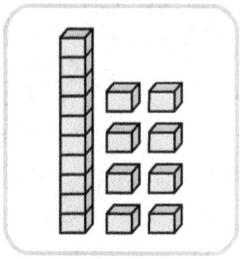

fifteen

16

Which square shows **12**?

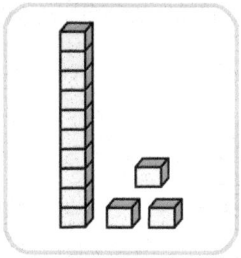

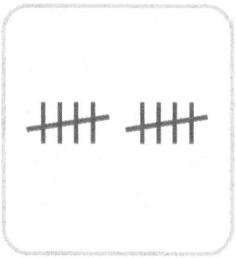

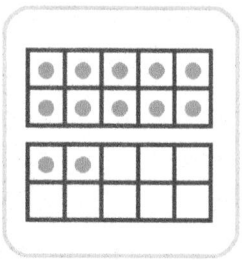

Which square shows **19**?

18

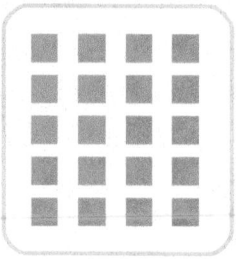

sixteen

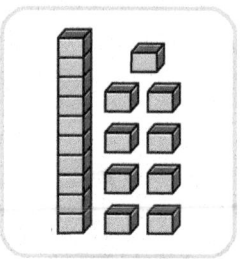

Which square shows **14**?

19

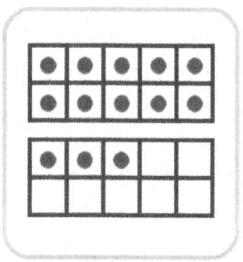

Chapter 3

Comparing Numbers

The puzzles in this chapter focus on comparing numbers. Your child will compare numbers up to 10 in the form of both numerals and groups of objects. By comparing the number of shells on sandcastles, spots on butterflies, or spikes on dinosaurs, your child will become familiar with terms such as *more than*, *less than*, *most*, *fewest*, and *same*. Some of the puzzles introduce the written symbols for *greater than* (>) and *less than* (<) as well as the *equal sign* (=).

Sandcastles

Draw lines to connect the sandcastles that have the **same** number of shells.

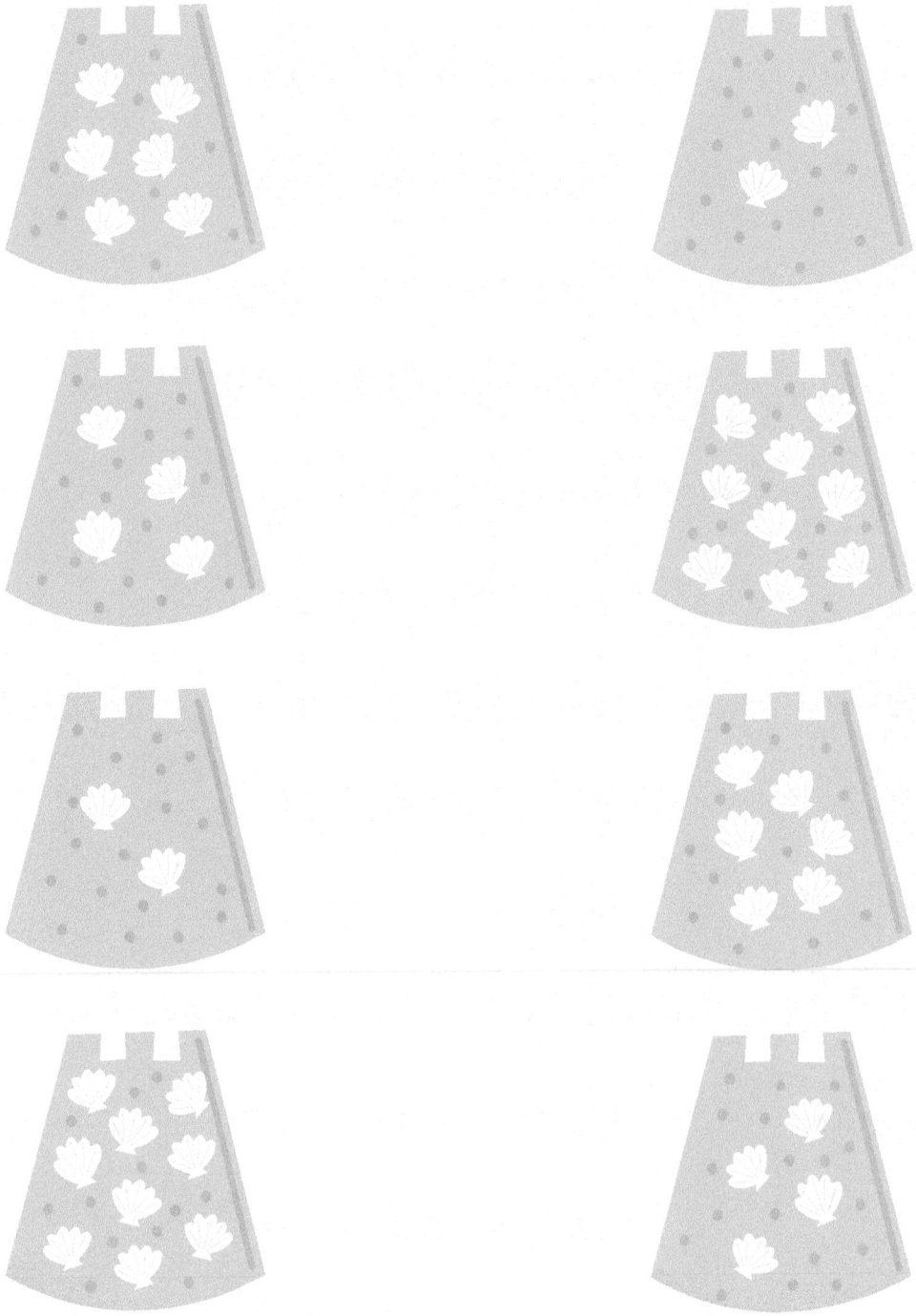

Peapods

Can you circle the peapods that have **more than 4** peas?

Butterflies

Here are two butterflies.

Can you decorate this butterfly so that it has **more** spots than its colorful friend?

Watermelon Seeds

Can you circle the watermelon slices that have **less than 8** seeds?

Which Dog?

Here are four dogs and four children. Draw a line to match each child to their pet dog.

Dinosaurs

Here are two dinosaurs.

Draw **6 more** spikes on this dinosaur.

Draw **5 more** spikes on this dinosaur.

Now count how many spikes each dinosaur has altogether.

Which dinosaur has **more** spikes? Color it green

Which dinosaur has **fewer** spikes? Color it orange

Number Pies

Here are four freshly baked number pies.
For each pie, write the **smallest** number in the box underneath.

Crocodiles

For each pair of numbers, circle the correct crocodile.
(And remember: The hungry crocodile always eats the **bigger** number.)

3 4

9 8

10 7

1 0

2 5

3 6

Compare these two numbers.
Can you draw your own crocodile symbol in the box?

8 6

Pizzas

Can you count and compare the number of mushrooms on each pair of pizzas?
Write >, <, or = in each box.

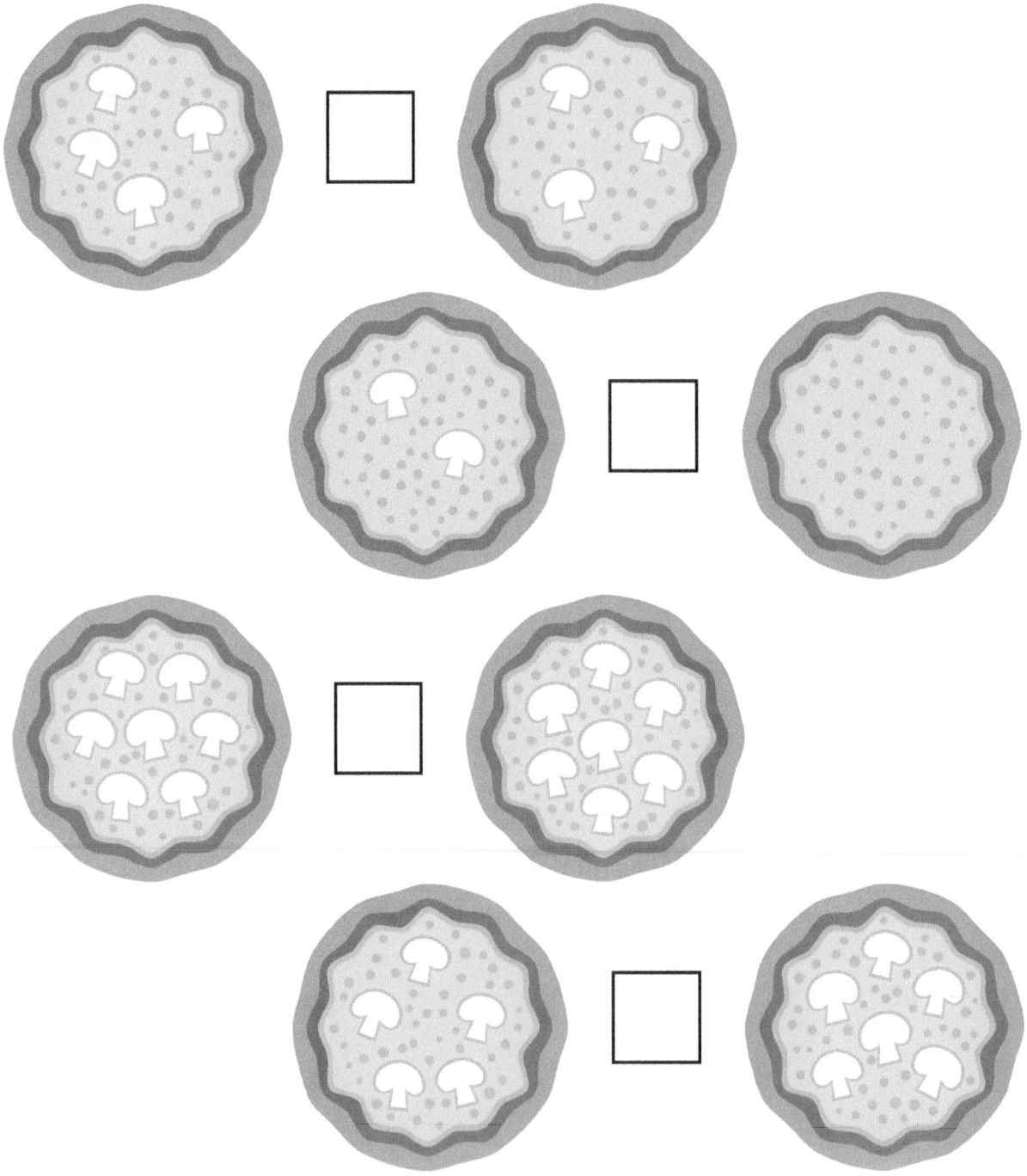

Marbles

Here are two jars full of colored marbles. Answer each question by coloring either **A** or **B**.

Which jar has **more** ? A B

Which jar has **more** ? A B

Which jar has **more** ? A B

Which jar has **more** ? A B

Storming the Castle

Look carefully at the picture. Are there more people **inside** the castle or **outside** the castle? Put a checkmark (✓) in the correct box.

There are more people:

inside the castle ☐ **outside** the castle ☐

Apples

Look at the number sentences in the apples. Some are **true** and some are **false.**
Can you color the ones that are **true**?

Chapter 4

Counting to 100

In this chapter, your child will have lots of practice at counting to 100. They will join numbers in order, find missing numbers, and decide what number should come next in a counting sequence. Some of the puzzles show a group of numbers at a time (for example, 20–30 or 40–60), while others use a hundreds chart so that children can see all numbers to 100 at once. At the end of this chapter, you will find puzzles that practice skip counting by 10—in one instance, by way of a group of party-loving penguins.

Houses

Look at the houses on the street.
Use the numbers on the front doors to help you answer the questions.

Which number comes after **22**?

Which number comes before **30**?

Which number comes after **24**?

Which number comes before **21**?

Which number comes after **29**?

Polly

Connect the dots in counting order from **1** to **35** to see who is sitting on the captain's shoulder.

Then color the picture.

Trains

Look at the numbers on each train.
Can you draw a line to the number that comes next?

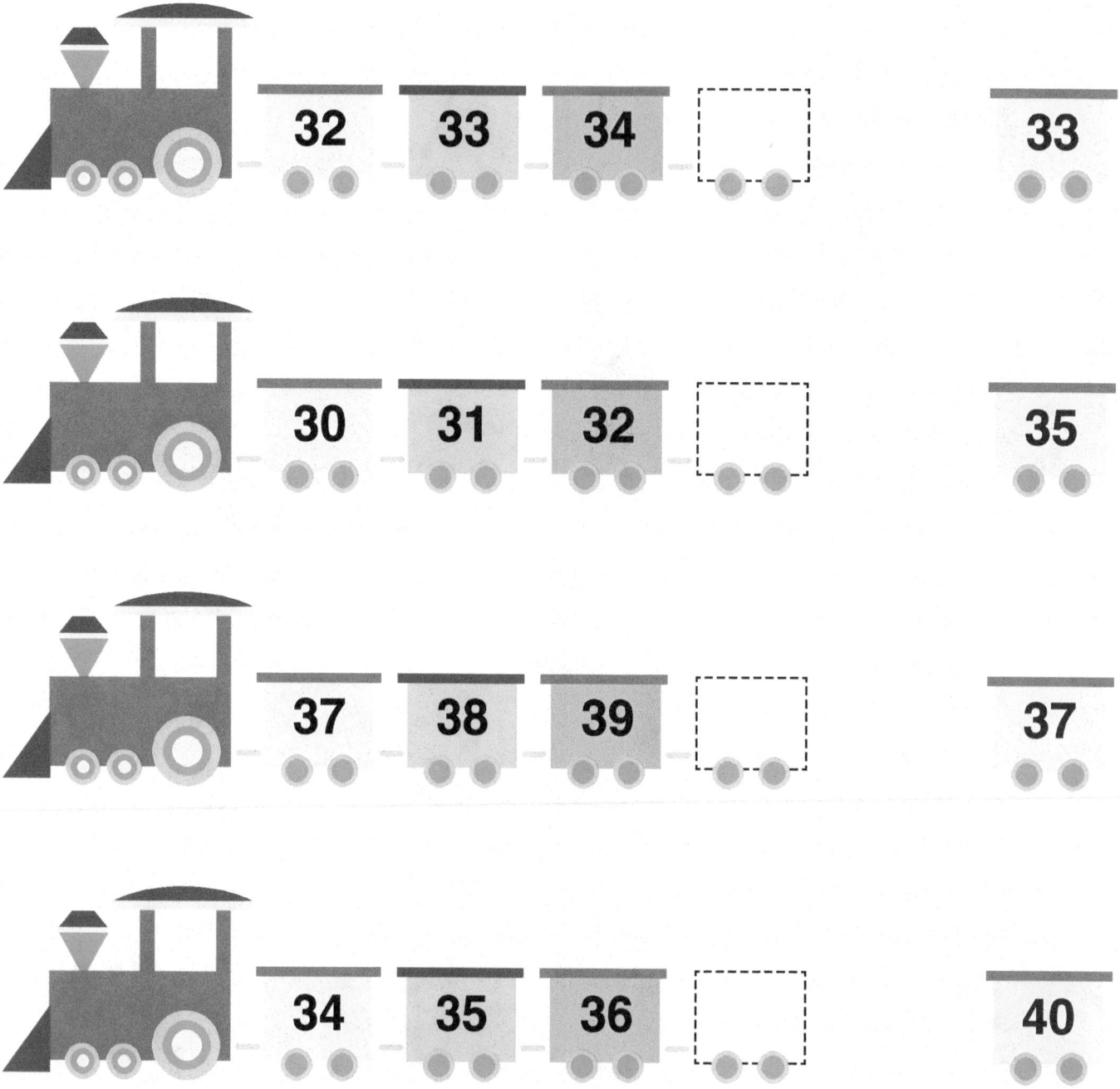

Caterpillars

Can you write the last number on each colorful caterpillar?

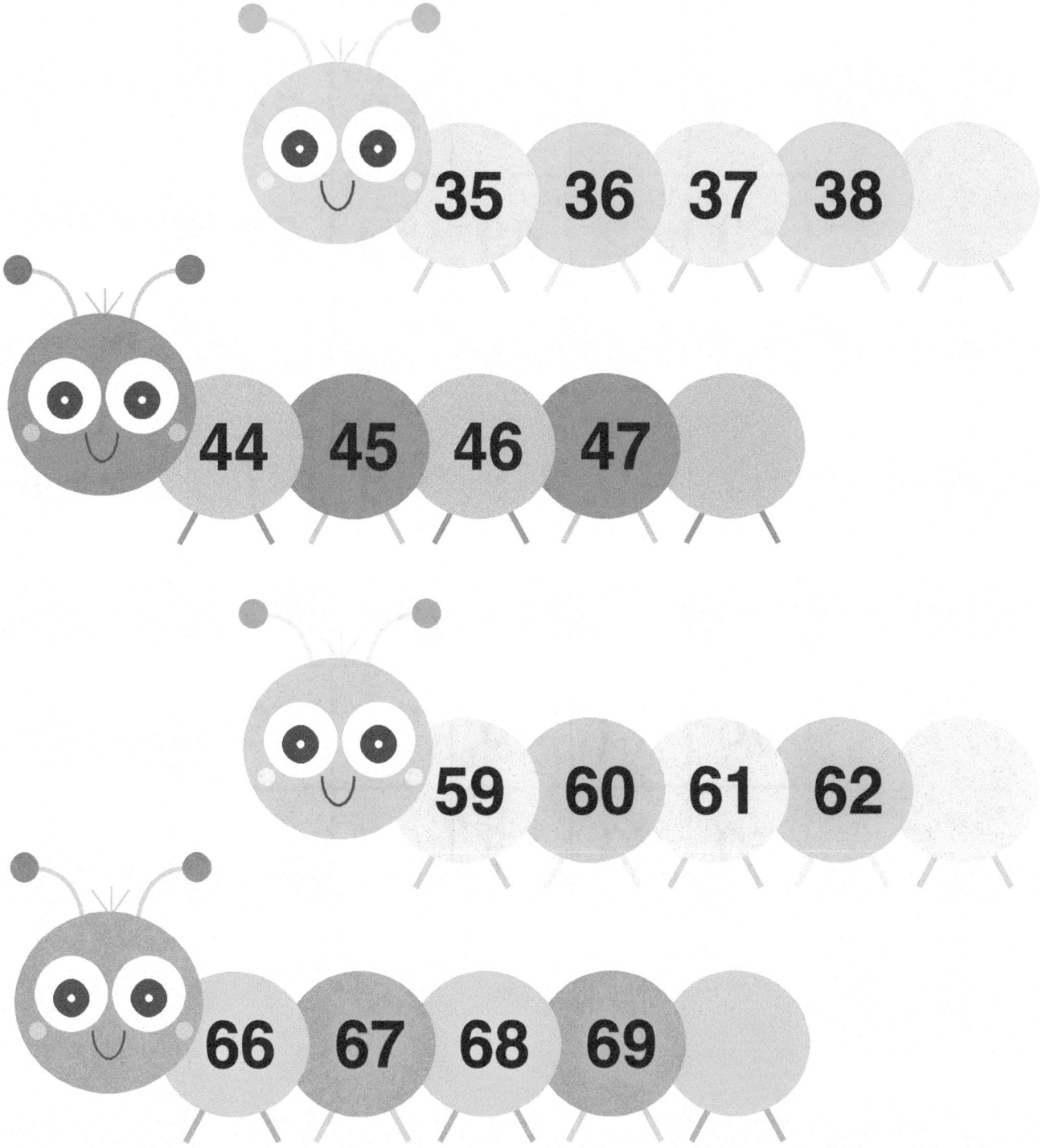

Bird's Nest

Which nest does the bird live in? Find the bird's home by following the numbers in order from **40** to **60**. Color the nest to show your answer.

40	41	45	53	52
50	42	49	50	51
59	43	44	45	46
51	50	49	48	47
52	53	54	44	58
48	49	55	56	59
60	59	58	57	60

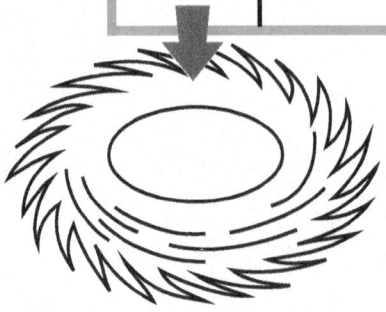

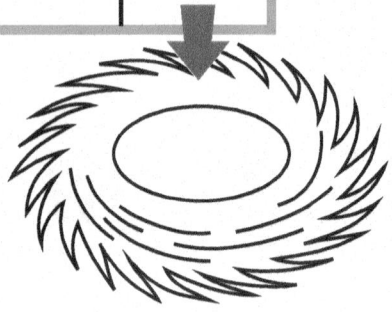

What's My Name?

Color these numbers on the hundreds chart to find out the missing letter of the girl's name: **14, 15, 16, 17, 18, 26, 36, 46, 54, 56, 64, 65, 66.** Write the letter on the line.

1	2	3	4	5	6	7	8	9	10
11	12	13	14	15	16	17	18	19	20
21	22	23	24	25	26	27	28	29	30
31	32	33	34	35	36	37	38	39	40
41	42	43	44	45	46	47	48	49	50
51	52	53	54	55	56	57	58	59	60
61	62	63	64	65	66	67	68	69	70
71	72	73	74	75	76	77	78	79	80
81	82	83	84	85	86	87	88	89	90
91	92	93	94	95	96	97	98	99	100

Up in the Sky

Can you connect the dots to find out what is flying in the sky? Start at **50** and count all the way to **70**. Then color the picture.

Paint Splatters

Oh, no! I've spilled paint on my page. Can you work out which numbers have been covered up? Write the missing numbers on the paint splatters.

1	2	3	4	5	6	7	8	9	10
11	12		14	15	16	17	18	19	20
21	22	23	24	25	26	27	28	29	30
31	32	33	34	35	36	37	38	39	40
	42	43	44	45	46	47	48	49	50
51	52	53	54	55		57	58	59	60
61	62	63	64	65	66	67	68	69	70
71	72	73	74	75	76	77	78	79	80
81		83	84	85	86	87	88	89	
91	92	93	94	95	96	97	98	99	100

Who's Swimming?

Connect the dots to see who is jumping out of the water. Start at **70** and count all the way to **100**. Then color the picture.

Counting Crayons

Each box has **10** crayons inside. For each group of boxes, count by **10** to see how many crayons there are altogether. Color the correct answer.

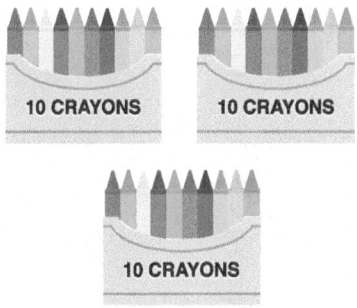

30 50 40

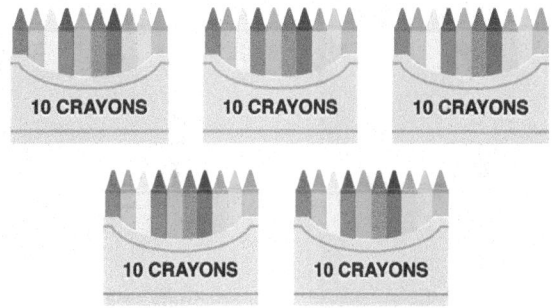

20 90 50

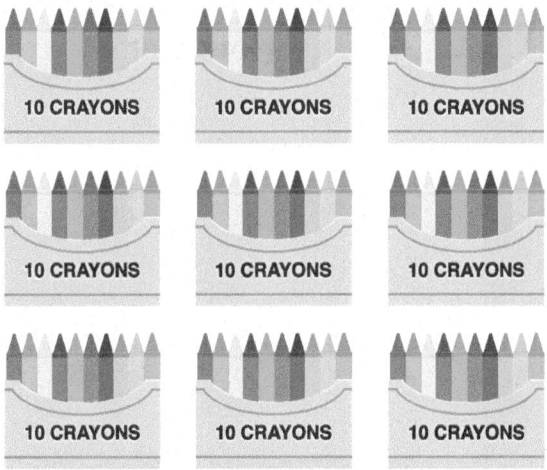

100 80 90

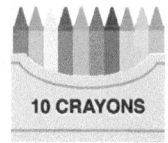

0 10 20

Party Penguins

The penguins are having a party!
Write the missing numbers on the penguins' party hats as you count by **10**.

Jumping Frog

Can you count by **10** to help the frog find the fly?
Starting at **10**, draw a line to show the correct path across the lily pads to **100**.

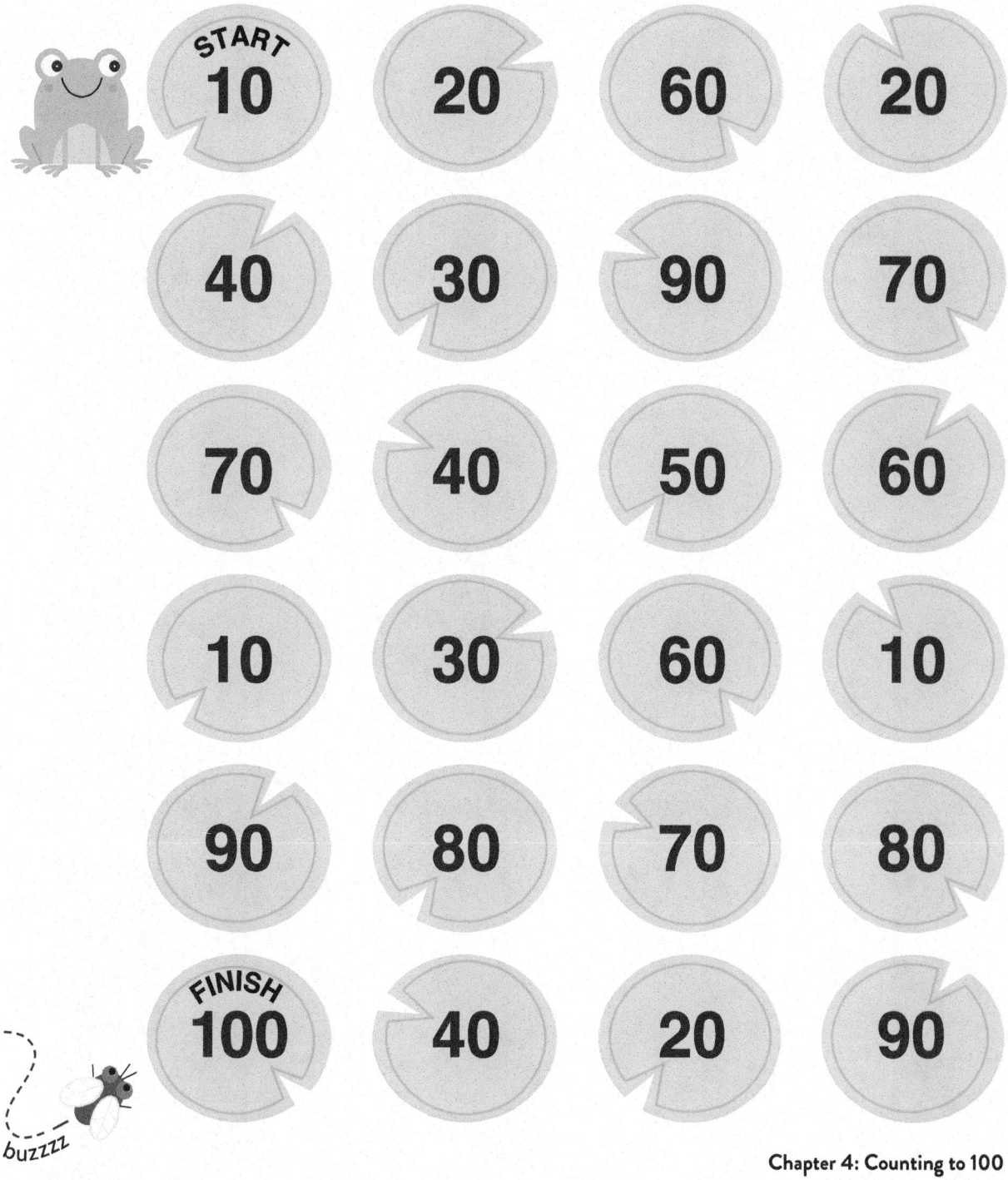

Chapter 5

Adding

At this age, children are introduced to addition as the idea of *putting numbers together.* You can help reinforce this concept with everyday practice using whatever is around you—toy cars, counters, or cookies on a plate. And puzzles add to the fun and learning. They start with addition within 5 before progressing to addition within 10. Here, you'll find picture addition puzzles (adding together groups of objects), number sentences, and simple word problems. Remind your child to use the pictures to help them with the puzzles. You could also have physical objects like blocks or pebbles on hand to count with.

Ducklings

Count the ducklings in each group. Add them together and write the number in the box.

Which Carrot?

Can you draw a line to match each rabbit to the correct carrot?

Sunflower

This sunflower has lots of leaves. Can you find the leaves with numbers that add up to **5**.

Color them **green**

Let's Play!

Count the balls in each group. Add them together and color the correct answer.

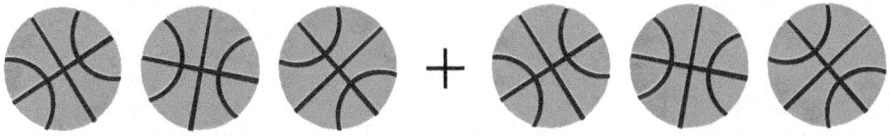

= 6 5 7

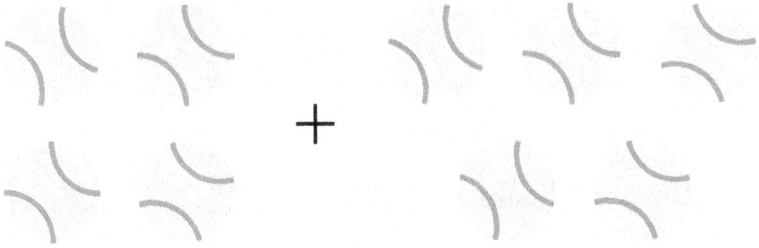

= 8 6 9

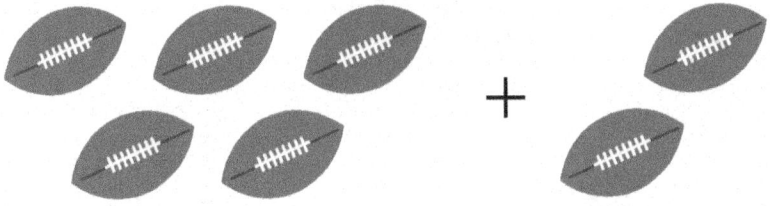

= 8 10 7

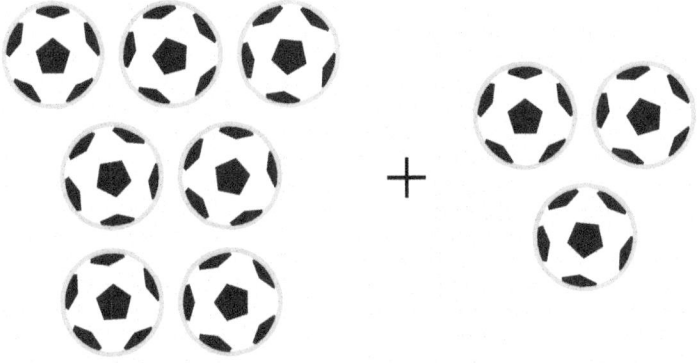

= 8 10 9

Library Books

At the library, I choose **4** books.

My sister chooses **5** books.

How many books do we take home altogether?

In the Rainforest

Who's sitting on the branch?
Solve the addition questions, and then use the code to color the picture.

1 = yellow 2 = white 3 = orange

4 = black 5 = green 6 = blue

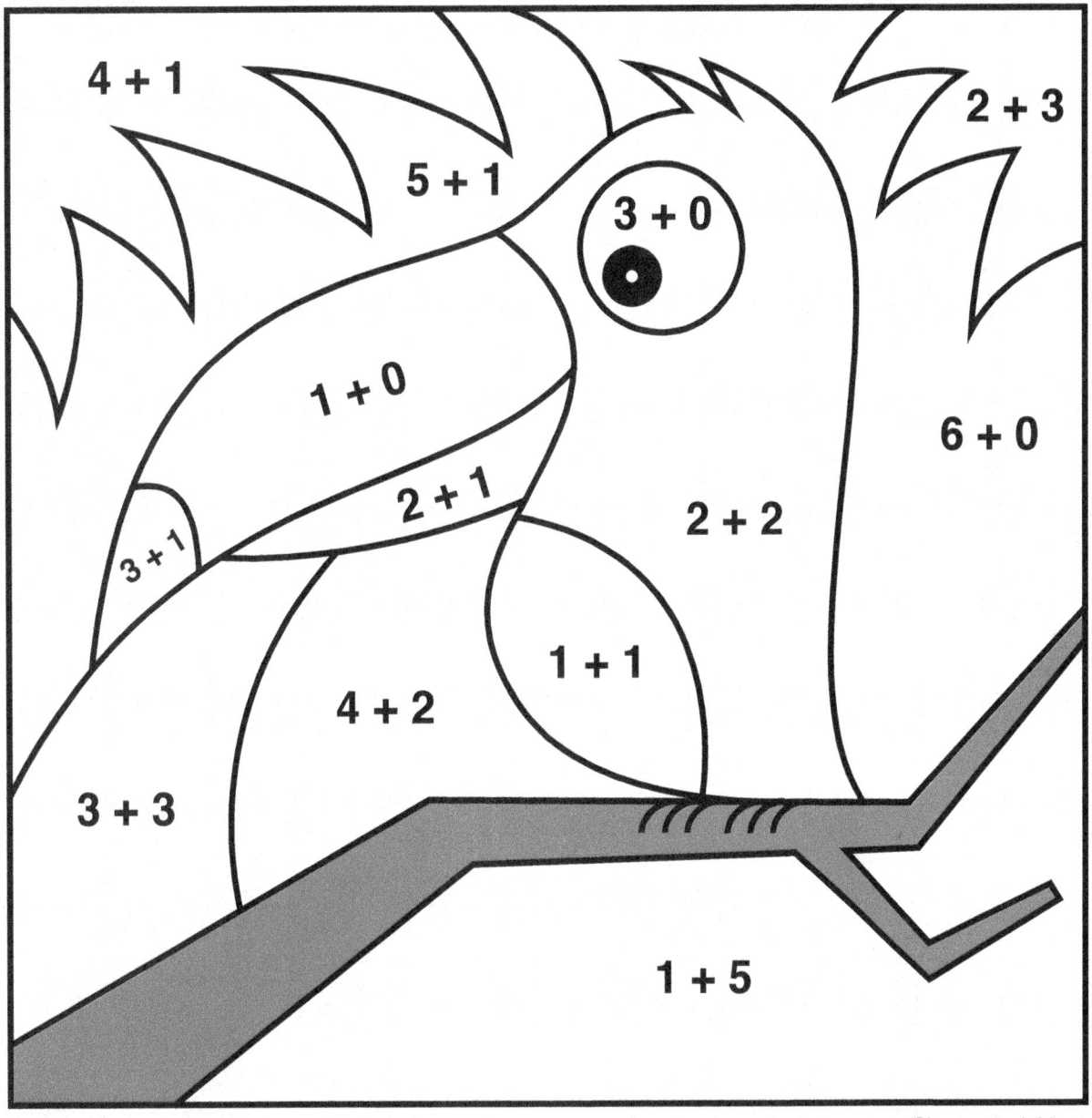

Dice

Add together the two numbers shown on the dice.
Then draw a line to the correct answer.

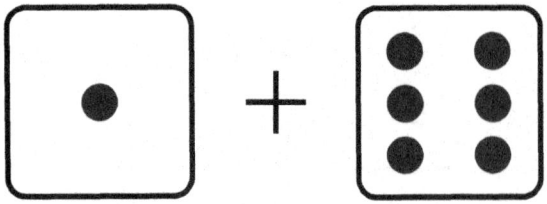

4

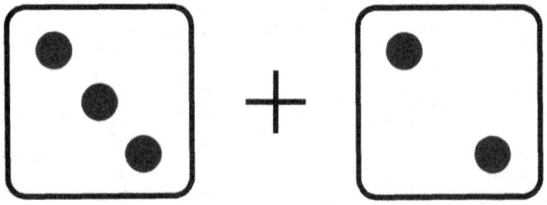

10

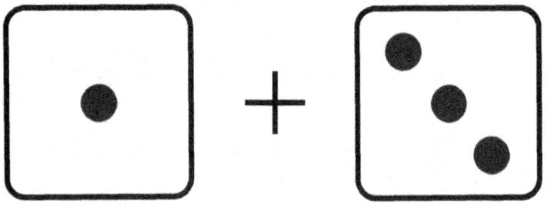

7

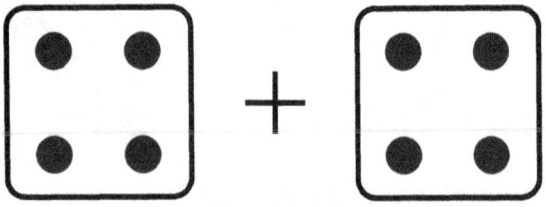

5

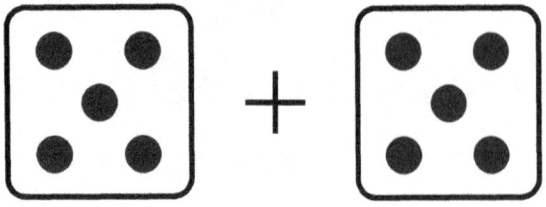

8

Hamburgers

There should be **10** hamburgers on my tray,
but my dog keeps taking them when I'm not looking!

For each tray below, count the hamburgers and write how many are missing.

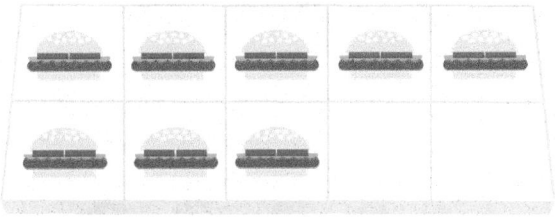

There are ☐ 🍔
There are ☐ missing

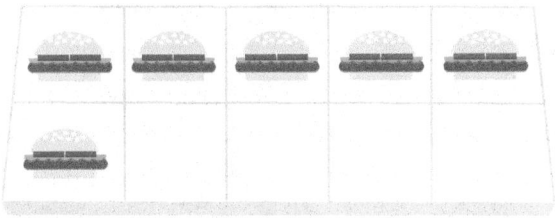

There are ☐ 🍔
There are ☐ missing

There are ☐ 🍔
There are ☐ missing

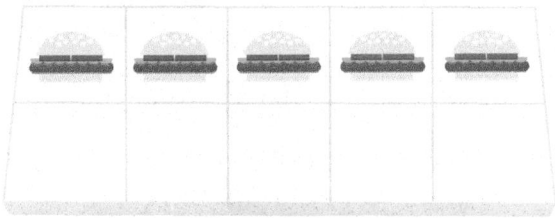

There are ☐ 🍔
There are ☐ missing

Strawberry Picking

Can you add together the numbers on each strawberry?
Draw a line to match each strawberry to the correct basket.

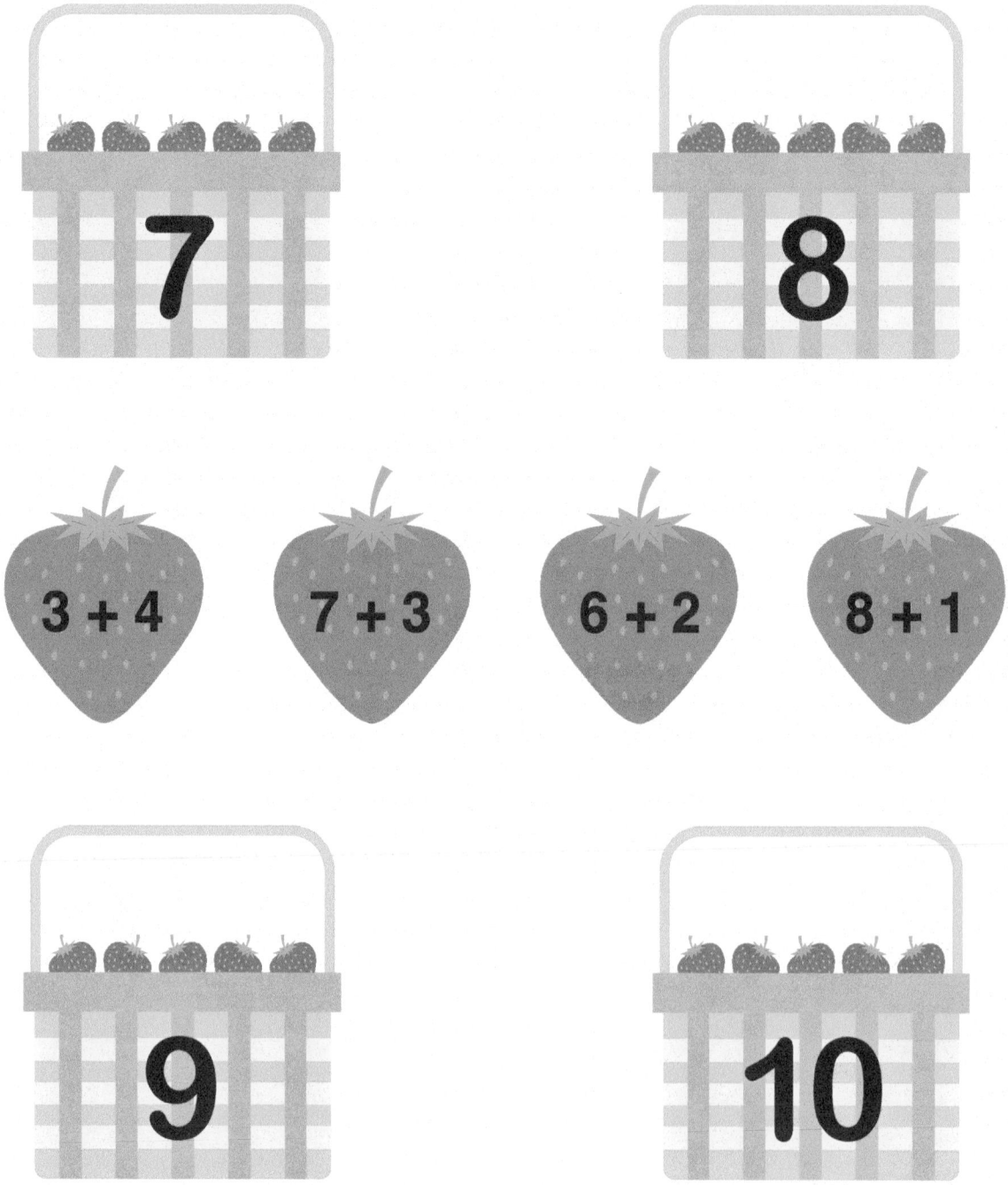

Twins

Here are five sets of twins. For each pair, can you make the numbers on the T-shirts add up to **10**? Fill in the number that's missing.

Hot-Air Balloons

Look at all the hot-air balloons.
Can you color all the hot-air balloons that add up to the number **9**?

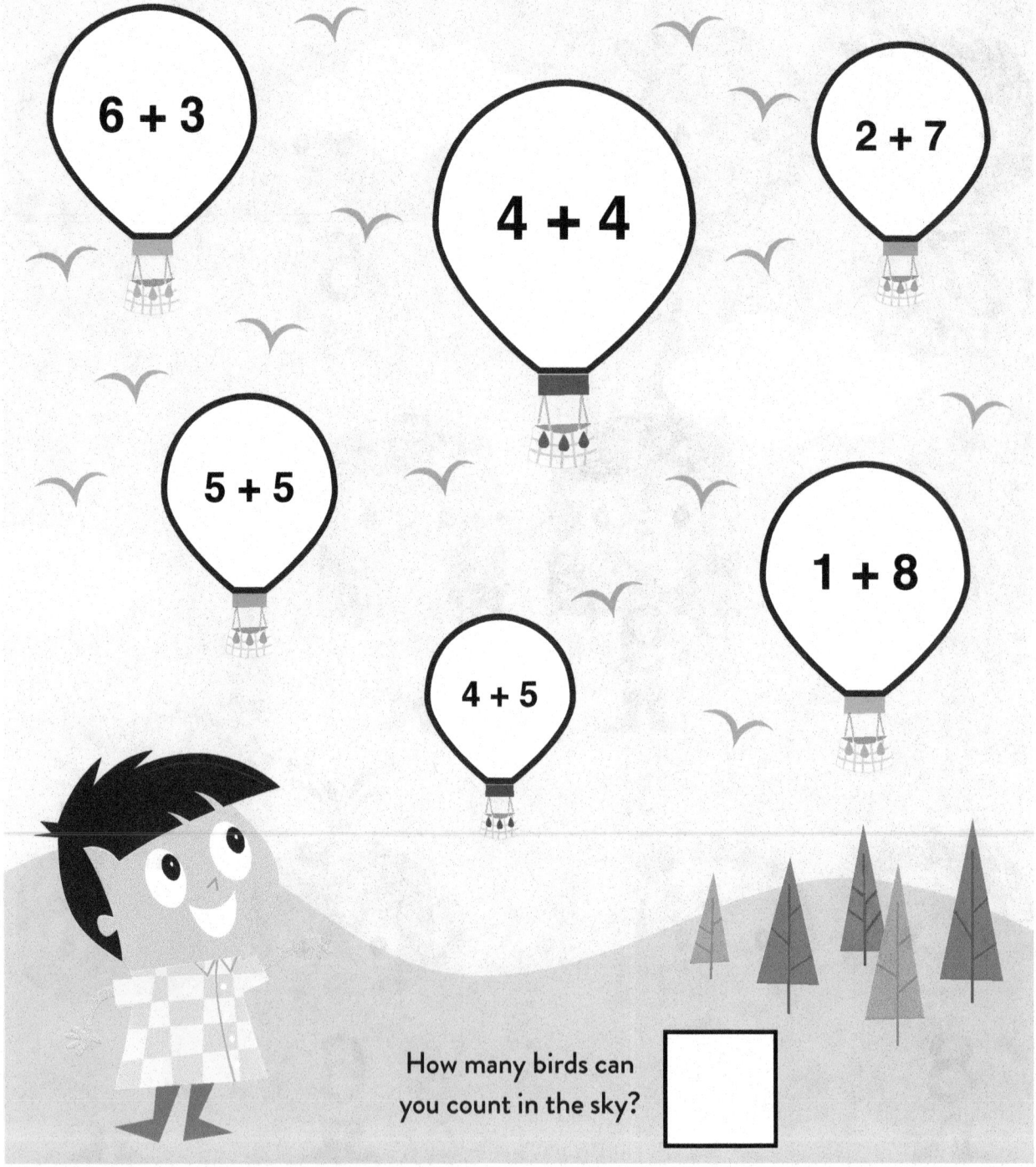

Chapter 6

Subtracting

As with addition, you can help your child learn the concept of subtraction using everyday items. In this chapter, your child will enjoy picture puzzles, puzzles with number sentences, and simple word problems. Themes like squirrels, the beach, and honey-loving bears make subtraction practice fun. When doing the picture puzzles, encourage your child to use the pictures to help them find their answer (for example, by crossing out the amount that is being subtracted). Also, you might find it helpful to use small objects to help reinforce the idea of *taking away*.

Fruit Salad

Cross out pieces of fruit to help you finish each number sentence.
Write your answer in the box.

4 – 1 = ☐

3 – 3 = ☐

5 – 4 = ☐

4 – 0 = ☐

At the Bakery

There are **5** loaves of bread for sale at the bakery.

A customer buys **2** loaves.

How many loaves are left? ☐

What treat do you like from the bakery? Draw it on the empty plate.

Hats

Look at all the different hats. Put a checkmark (✓) next to all the hats that have the answer **2.**

Squirrels

Can you draw a line to match each squirrel to the correct acorn?

Bears and Honey

These bears are hungry! For each question, cross out the number of honey jars the bear has eaten. Then write how many jars are left in the box.

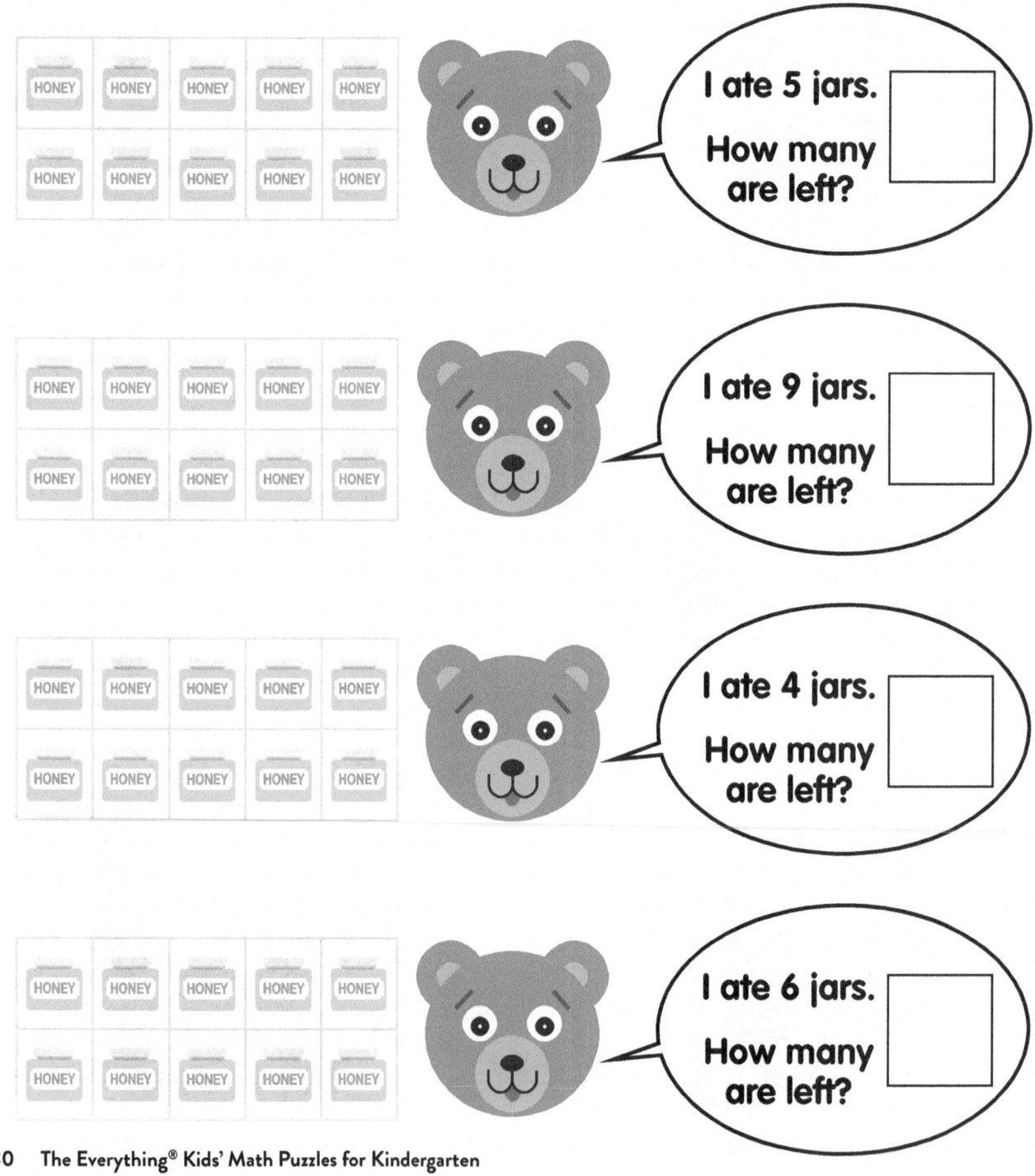

Bees

There are **7** bees near the hive.

3 bees fly away to collect some pollen.

How many bees are left? ☐

Fishing

This girl is busy fishing.

Can you color all the fish that have the answer **4**?

On the Beach

It's a beautiful day at the beach.
Answer the subtraction questions, and then use the code to color the beach objects.

1 = orange 2 = green 3 = blue

4 = red 5 = purple 6 = yellow

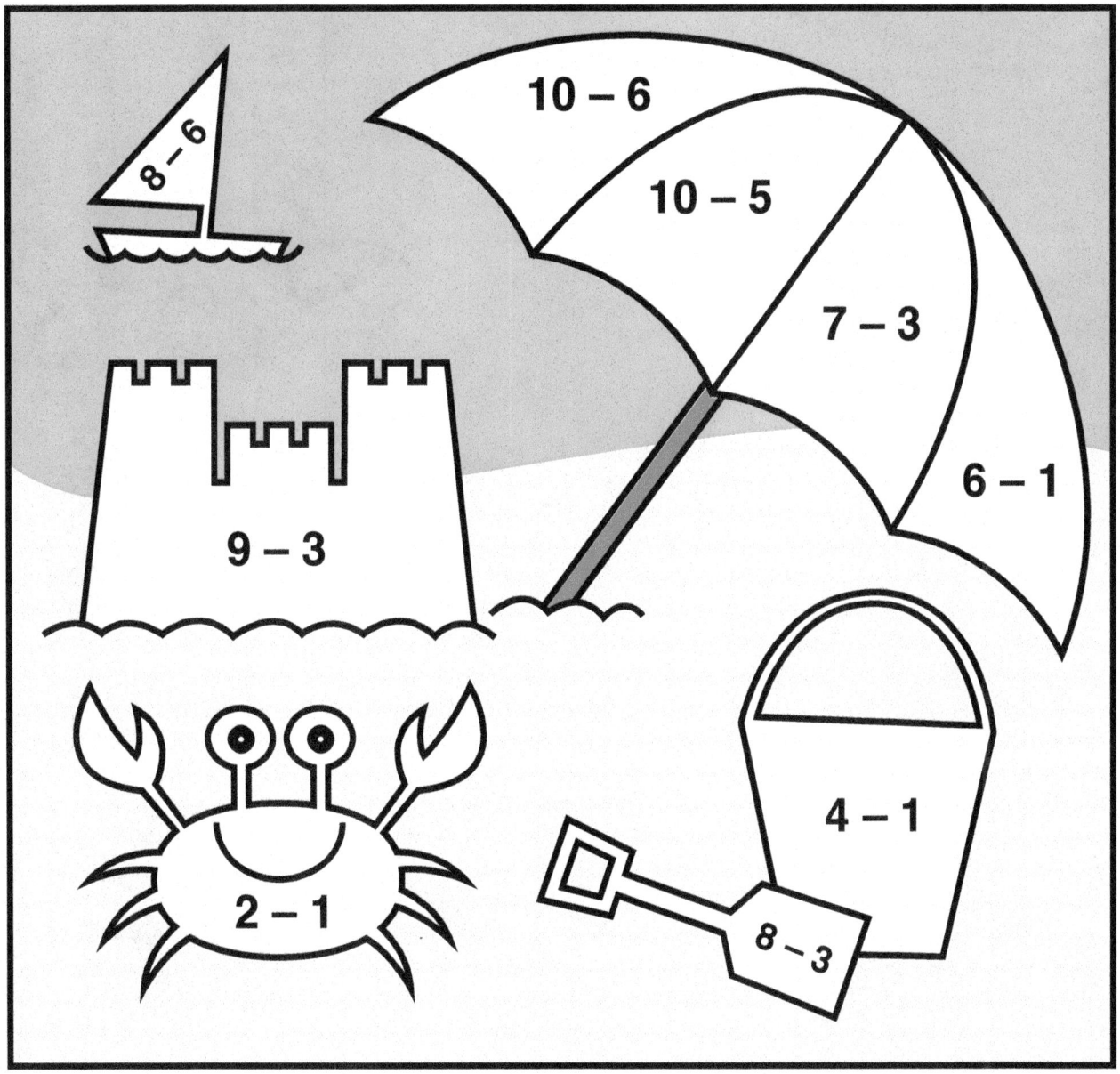

Flying Saucers

Can you draw a line to match each flying saucer to the correct planet?

Happy or Sad?

Look at these number sentences. Some of them are right and some are wrong.
If the number sentence is right, color the happy face. If it is wrong, color the sad face.

$10 - 3 = 6$

$9 - 6 = 3$

$8 - 6 = 4$

$9 - 1 = 8$

$10 - 8 = 2$

Chapter 7

Measurement and Data

Measurement puzzles focus on attributes such as height, length, width, and capacity. These activities will help your child practice comparing two (or sometimes more) objects in terms of these attributes. For example, they may have to decide which wiggly worm is longer, which backyard object is heavier, or which snowman is the tallest. This chapter will also give your child practice at sorting things according to their properties, such as size, color, or number of legs.

Which Animal?

Can you draw a line to match each description to the correct animal?

This animal is tall with a long neck.

This animal is small and light.

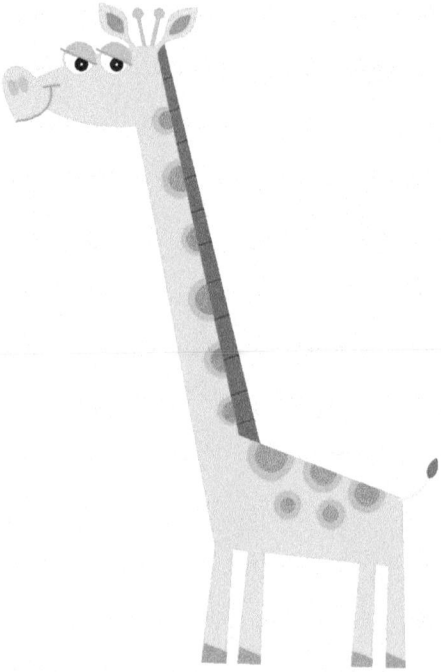

This animal is big and heavy.

Sorting Socks

Can you help sort the socks?

Color the socks with spots **blue** Color the socks with stripes **yellow**

How many **blue** socks are there?

How many **yellow** socks are there?

Legs

Can you sort these creatures into those that have **4** legs and those that don't? Draw a line from each creature to the correct label.

Has 4 legs

Does not have 4 legs

Snowmen

Look at the three cheery snowmen.
Answer the questions below by writing **A**, **B**, or **C** in the box.

Which snowman is the **tallest**?

Which snowman is the **shortest**?

Which snowman has the **most** buttons?

Which snowman has the **biggest** hat?

In the Backyard

For each pair of objects, can you circle the one that would be **heavier**?

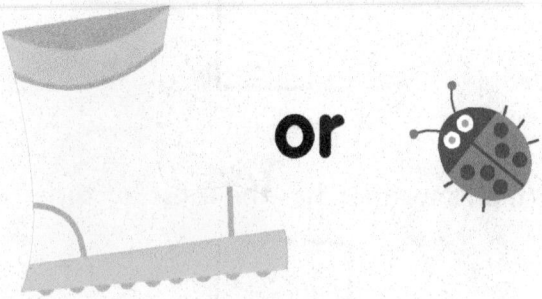

Pairs

Here are four pairs of objects. For each pair, can you put a checkmark (✓) next to the one that is **shorter**?

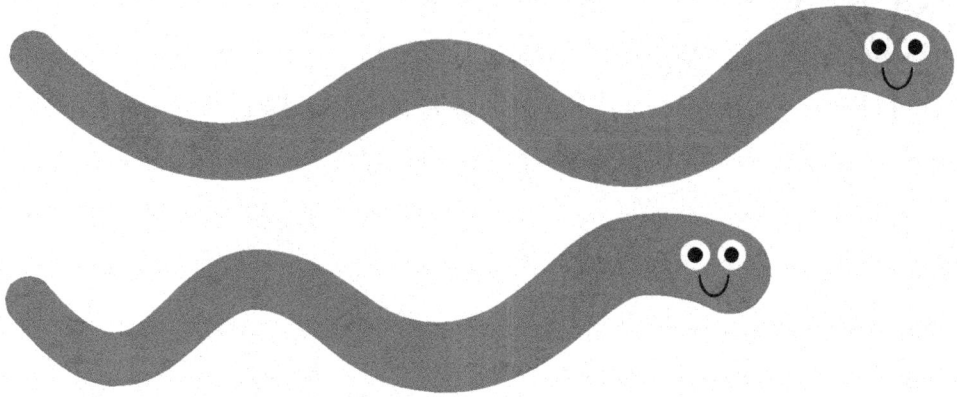

Gifts

Look at each set of gifts. For each question, color your answer.

Color the gift that is **widest.**

Color the gift that is **tallest.**

Color the gift that is **smallest.**

On the Move

The pictures on this page show different ways of getting from one place to another. Some of the pictures show things with wheels and some show things without wheels.

Circle the things **with wheels** in green Circle the things **with no wheels** in red

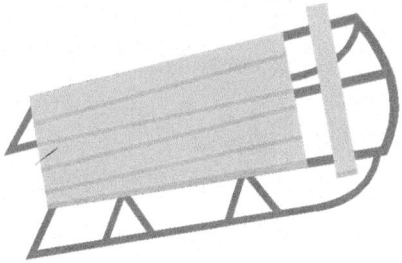

Pencil Case

Can you count how many blocks long each object is?

Put a checkmark (✓) next to the **longest** object.

Put a smiley face ☺ next to the **shortest** object.

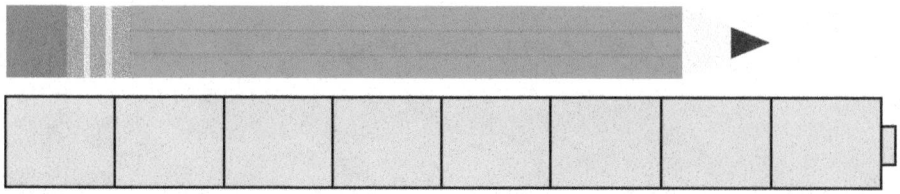

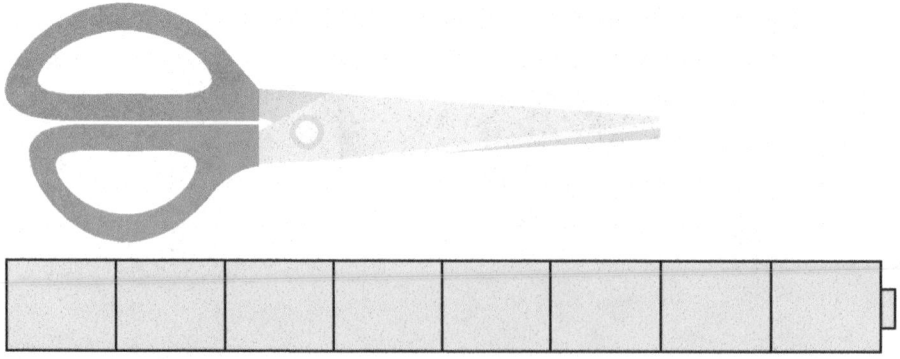

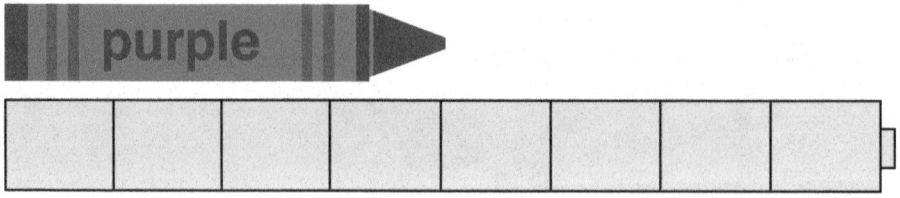

Enchanted Forest

Look at all the toadstools in the enchanted forest.

Color the **big** toadstools red Color the **small** toadstools purple

Are there more red or purple toadstools?
Check the correct box.

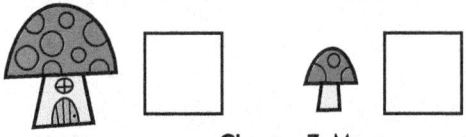

Water

Look at the three containers on the table.
Answer the questions by writing **A**, **B**, or **C** in the box.

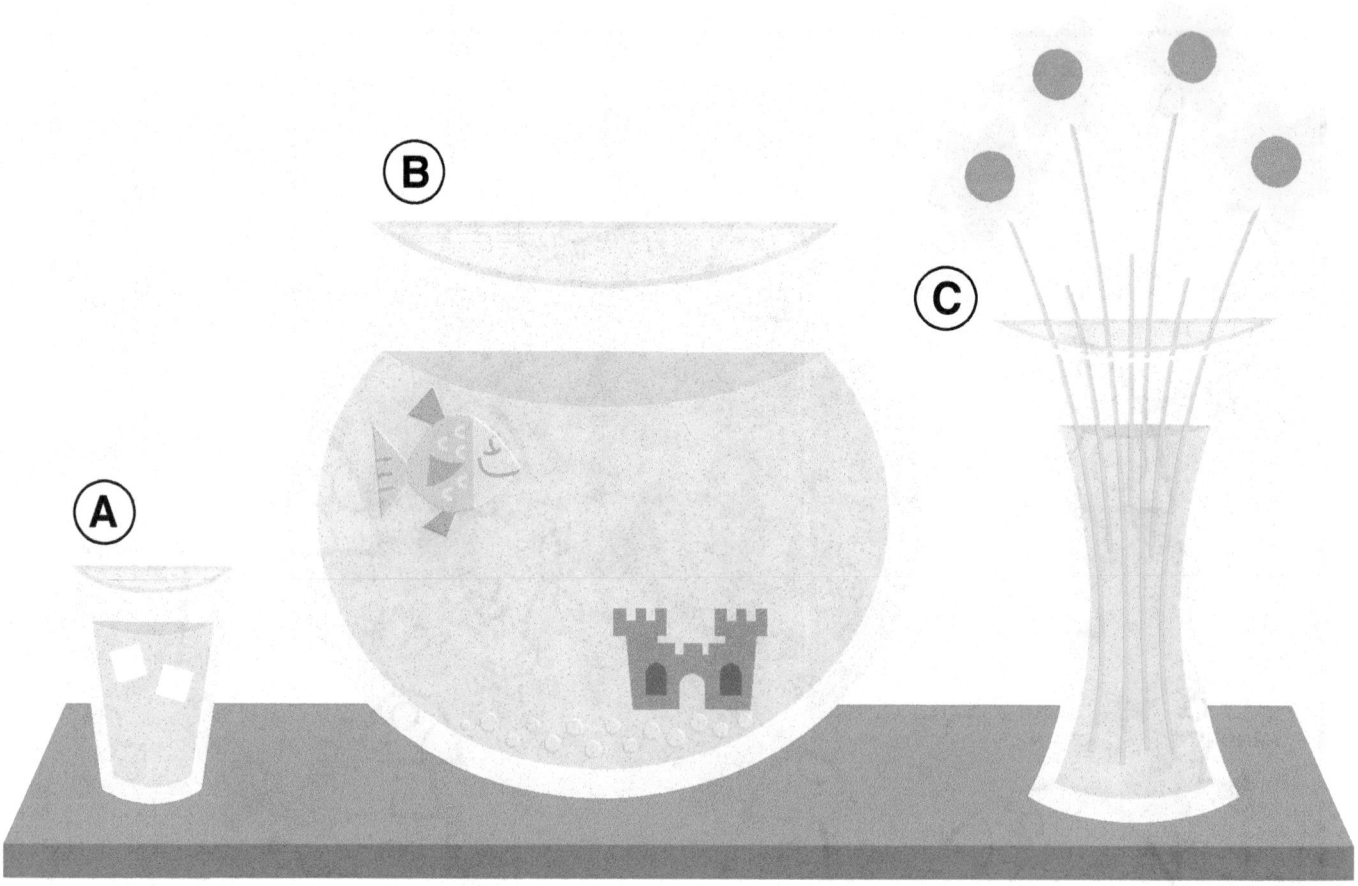

Which container holds the **most** water? ☐

Which container holds the **least** water? ☐

Can you add **1** more ice cube, **2** more fish, and **3** more flowers to the picture?

How's the Weather?

The clothes have been sorted into two groups: warm weather clothes and cold weather clothes. Unfortunately, there are some mistakes. Can you circle the clothes that are in the wrong group?

Jelly Beans

Can you count the different colored jelly beans?
Color the blocks on the chart to show how many of each color there are.

	red	yellow	green	purple
5				
4				
3				
2				
1				

Chapter 8

Shapes and Patterns

The shape puzzles in this chapter feature both two-dimensional (2-D) and three-dimensional (3-D) shapes. Your child will practice identifying and naming these shapes, spotting them in different scenarios, and sorting them according to their type and properties (such as number of sides, faces, or corners). In addition to shape puzzles, this chapter includes puzzles about position words (such as *in front of*, *next to*, and *inside*). Pattern puzzles ask your child to continue or complete simple repeating patterns made with shapes and colors.

Everyday Shapes

Can you draw a line to match each object to the correct shape?

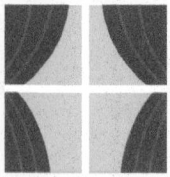

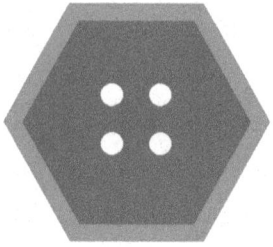

triangle

hexagon

rectangle

circle

square

Mice and Cheese

Mice love cheese! For each row, circle the picture that matches the sentence.

The mouse is <u>inside</u> the cheese.

The mouse is <u>in front of</u> the cheese.

The mouse is <u>on top of</u> the cheese.

The mouse is <u>next to</u> the cheese.

Jewels

Look at the patterns made by the sparkly jewels.
For each pattern, can you draw the shape that comes next?

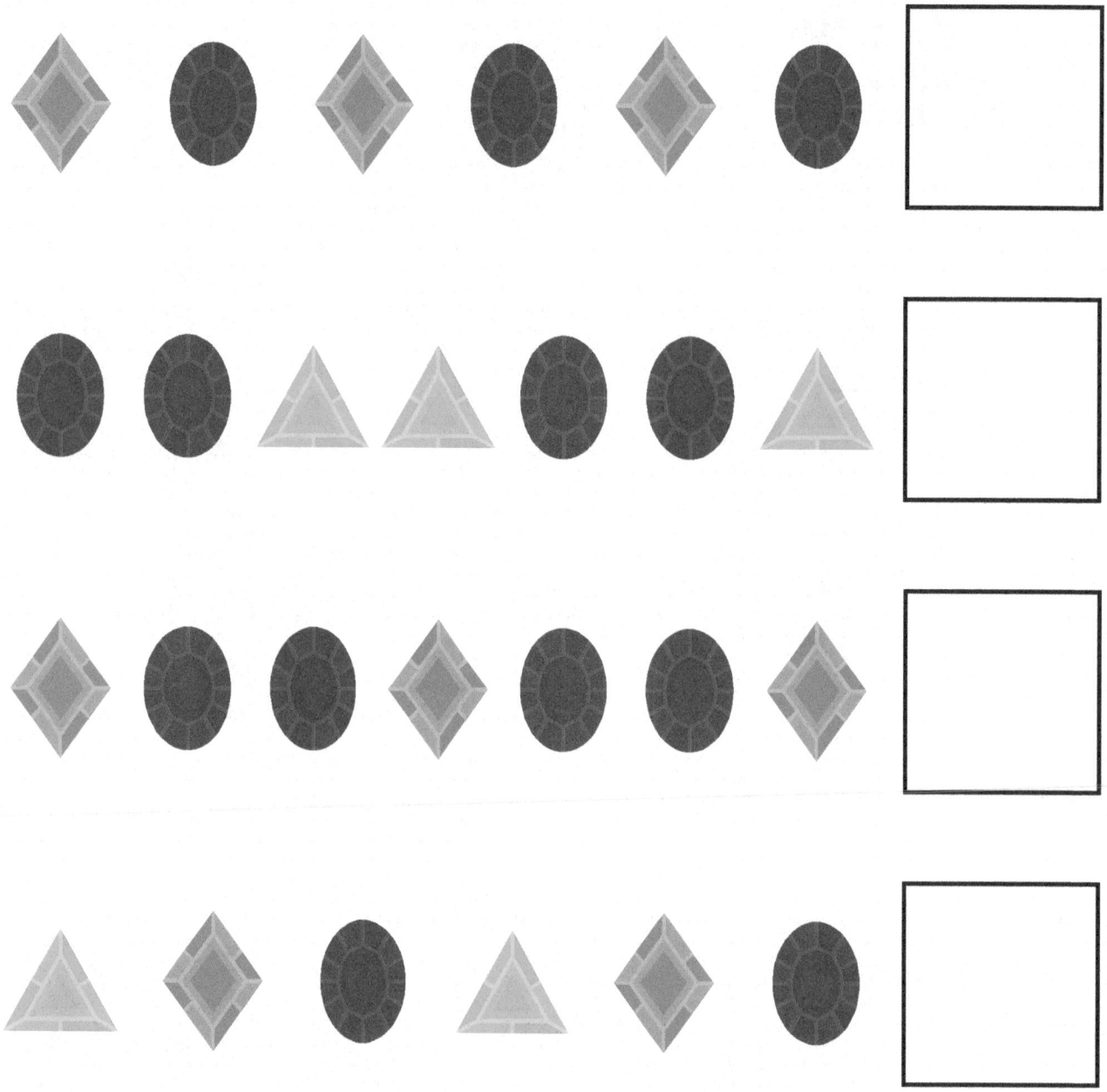

Design a Hat

Can you decorate this hat using shapes? Color it to make it bright and colorful.

Kites

Look at the shapes on the children's kites.
Match each kite to the correct child by writing **A**, **B**, **C**, or **D** in each box.

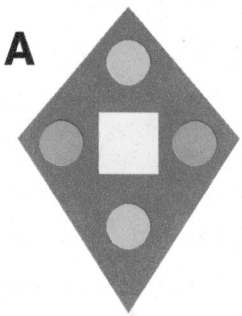

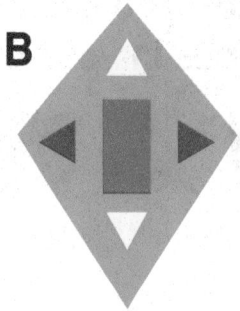

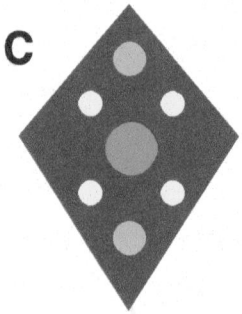

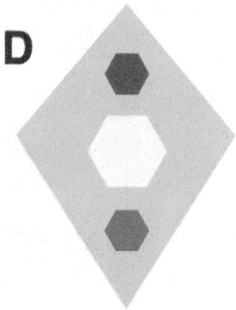

My kite has 3 hexagons.

My kite has 7 circles.

My kite has 4 circles and 1 square.

My kite has 1 rectangle and 4 triangles.

Robot

This robot is made of different shapes.

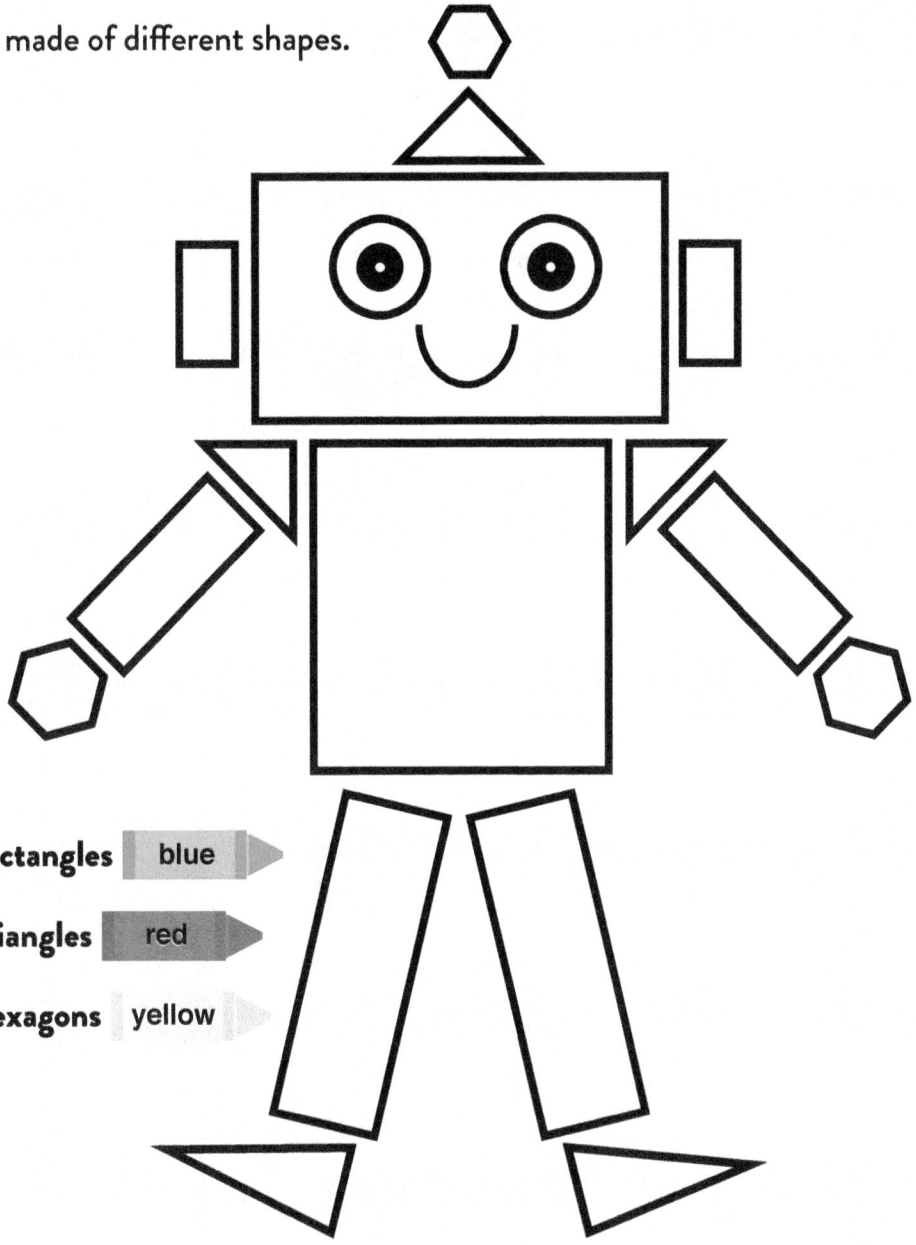

Color the **rectangles** blue

Color the **triangles** red

Color the **hexagons** yellow

Can you count the different shapes? Write the numbers in the boxes.

rectangles **triangles** **hexagons**

Cookies

These children want to tell you about their cookies.
Look at each cookie on the tray, and write **A**, **B**, **C**, or **D** in each box.

My cookie has 3 corners.

My cookie has 4 sides that are all the same length.

My cookie has no corners.

My cookie has 4 sides. 2 sides are long and 2 sides are short.

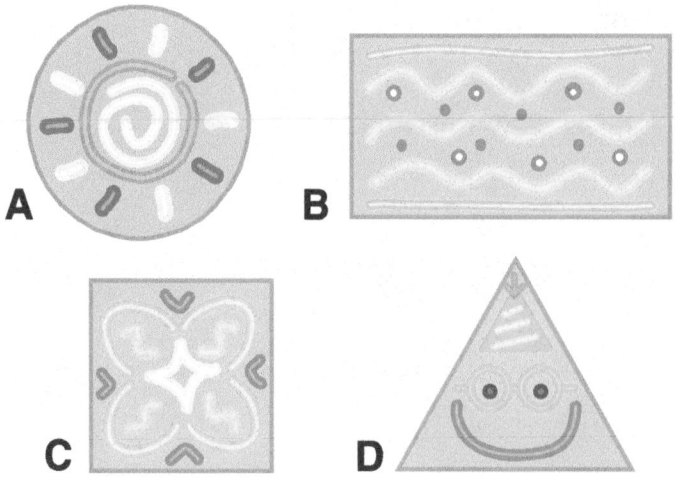

Shape Pictures

Shapes can join together to make pictures.
Draw a line to match each picture to the shapes you would need to build it.

Pictures

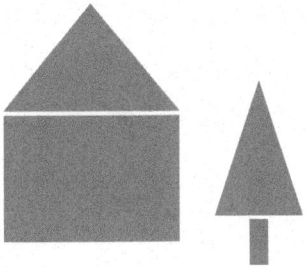

Shapes

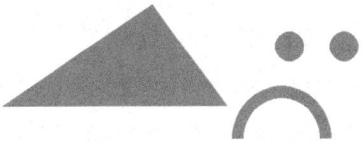

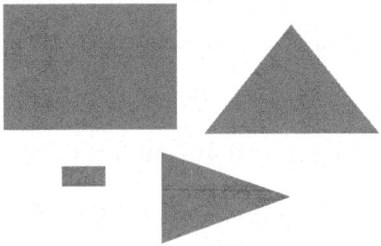

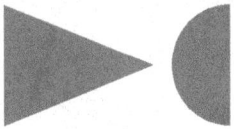

Flat or Solid?

Some of these shapes are **flat** (2-D) and some are **solid** (3-D).

Color all the **flat** shapes red

Color all the **solid** shapes blue

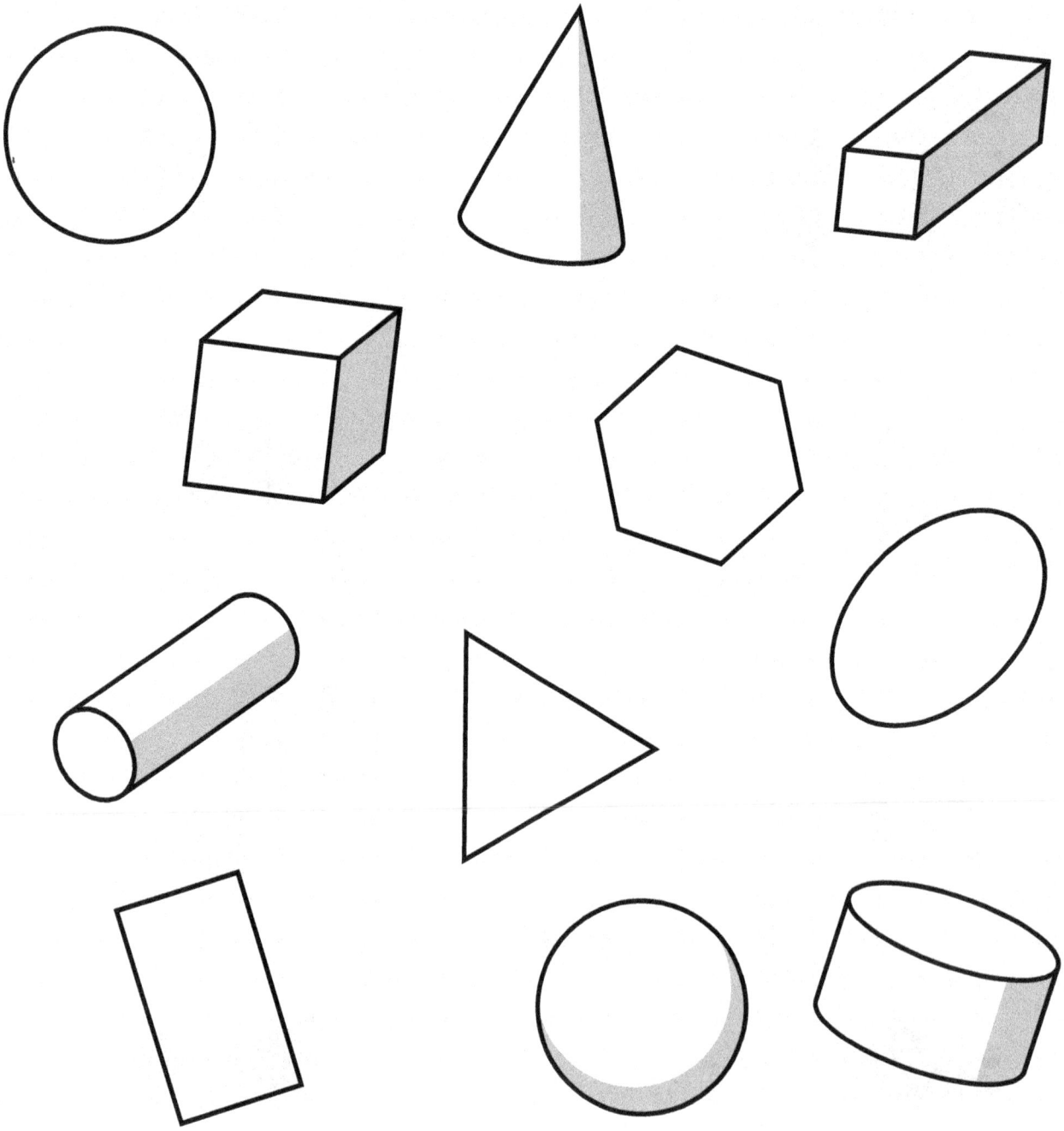

Shape People

Look at these shape people. They are each a different solid shape.
Can you draw a line to match each shape person to the correct shape name?

sphere

cylinder

cone

cube

Traffic Light

Look at the long line of cars waiting at the red light.
Continue the color pattern by coloring the last four cars.

How many **blue** cars are there now?

Shapes All Around

This boy is busy drawing a picture. Look at the objects around his room. There are a lot of solid shapes to spot. Find and circle:

5 cylinders red **3** spheres blue **4** cubes green

Toy Store

Look at the toys on the shelves.
For each sentence, color the box that makes the sentence true.

The  is **in front of** / **beside** the 

The  is **above** / **below** the 

The  is **behind** / **beside** the 

The  is **below** / **above** the 

There is a mouse hiding **behind** one of the toys. Can you spot it and circle it?

What Am I?

For each clue, can you circle the correct shape?

I am a solid shape.
I have 6 square faces.

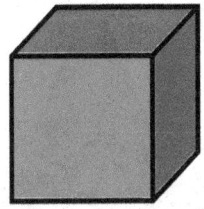

or

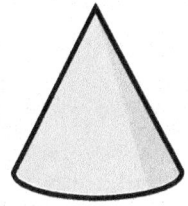

I am a flat shape.
I have 6 sides.

or

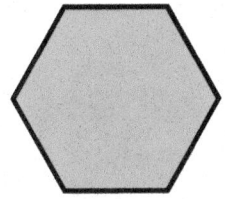

I am a solid shape.
I have no corners.

or

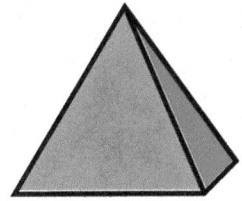

I am a flat shape.
I have 4 sides and
4 corners.

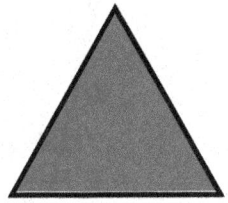

or

Cone or Cylinder?

Can you sort the shapes into **cones** and **cylinders**?
Draw a line to match each shape to the correct shape name.

cylinder

cone

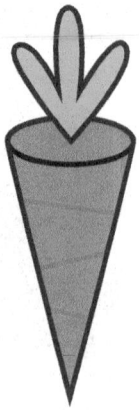

What Is Missing?

Look at the four different shape patterns. In each pattern, there is a **?** where a shape is missing. Can you circle the missing shape?

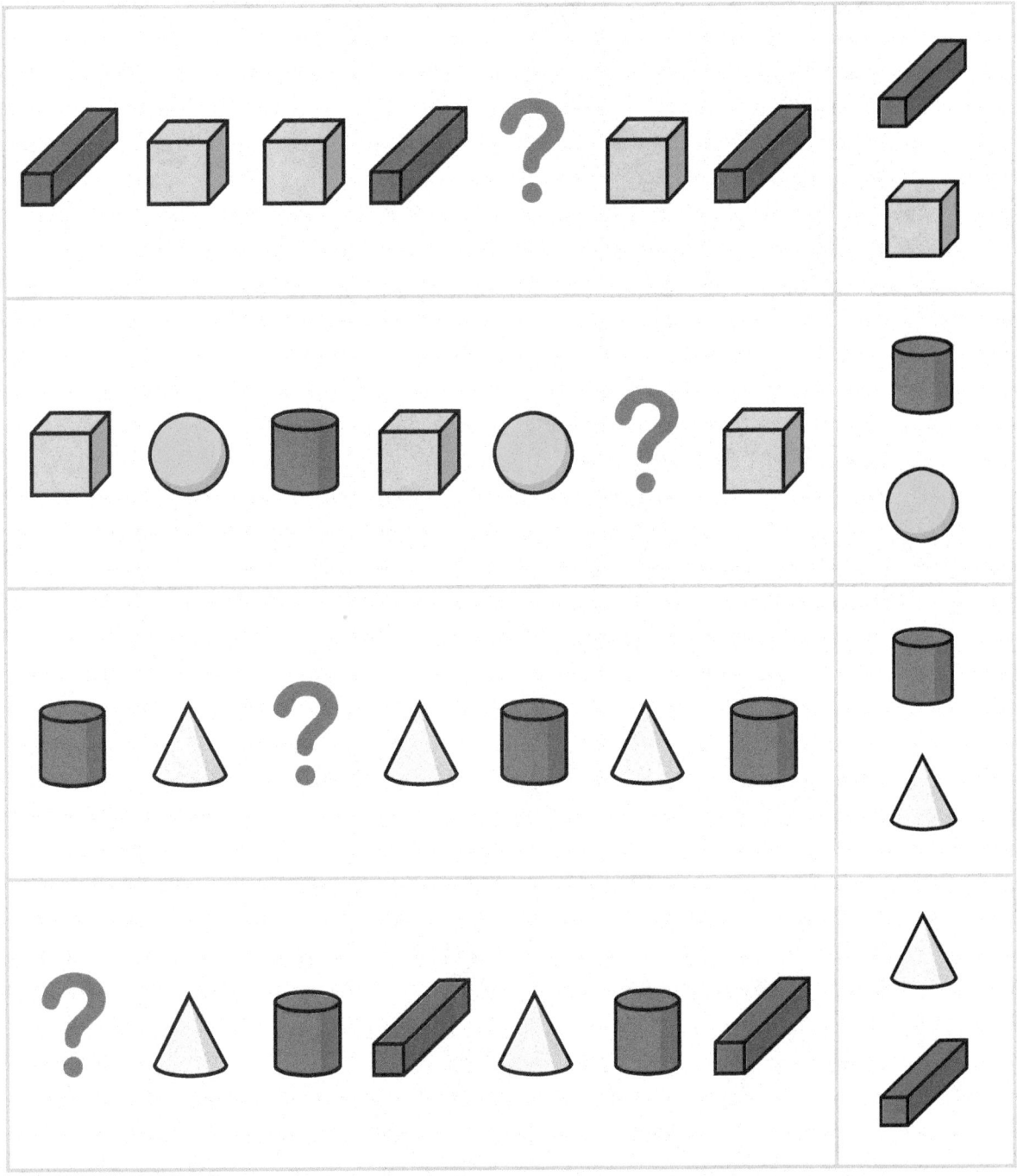

Answers

Chapter 1

Page 8 • Ice Cream

Page 9 • Under the Sea

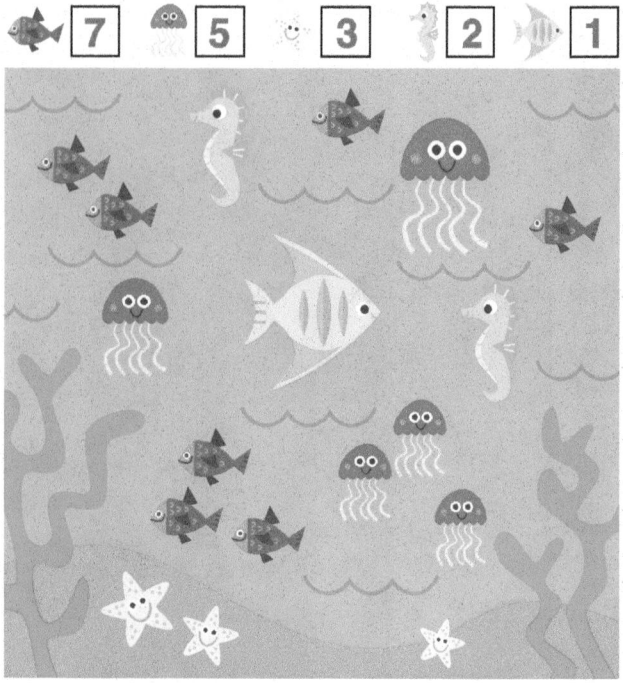

Page 10 • Goldfish Bowls

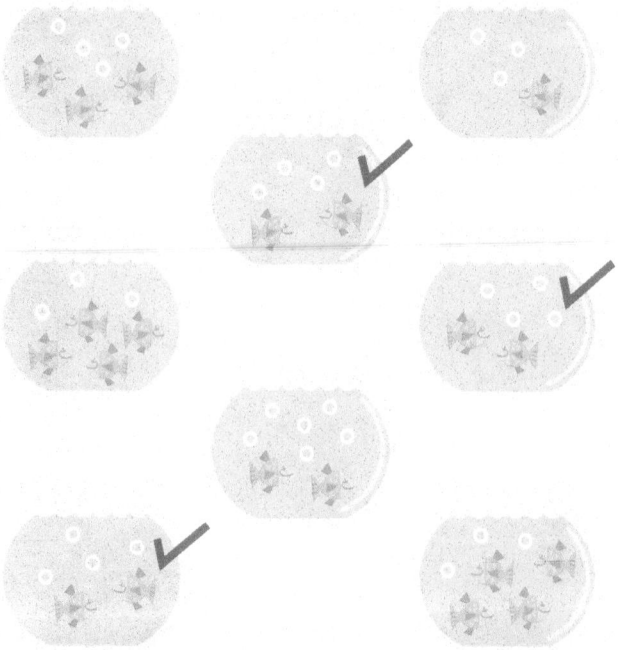

Page 11 • Space Aliens

Your drawing here

Page 12 • Counting Raindrops

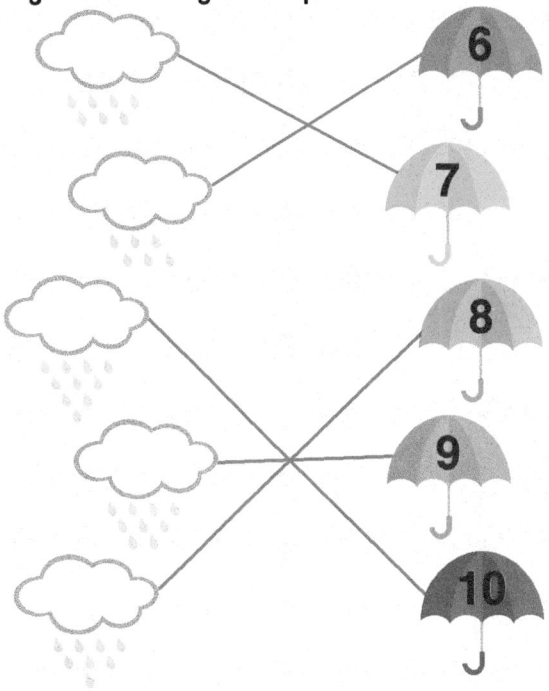

Page 13 • School Buses

Page 14 • Birthday Cake

Page 15 • Ladybugs

Page 16 • Countdown

Page 17 • Bubbles of 10

Page 18 • Find the Fish

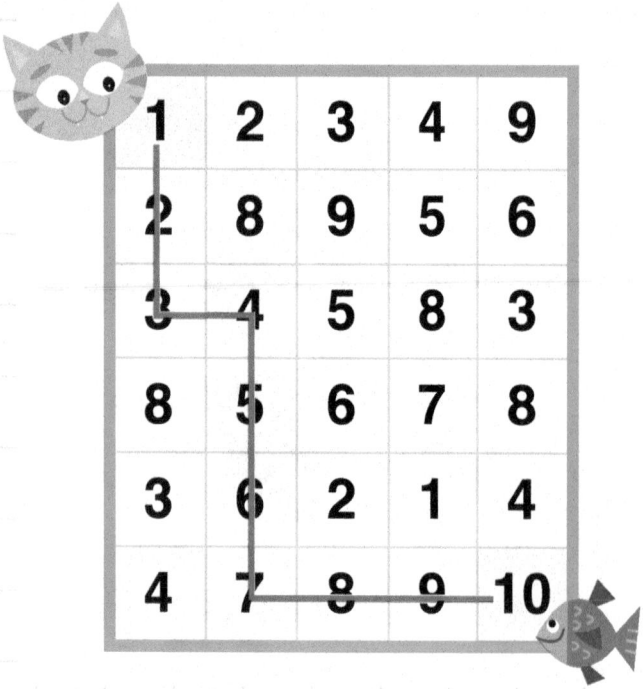

Page 19 • Scarves

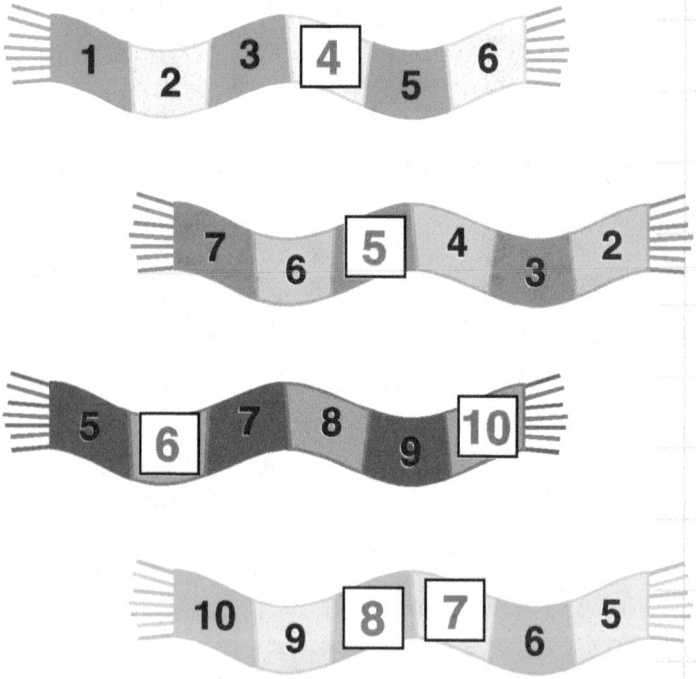

Chapter 2

Page 20 • Number Squares (Numbers to 10)

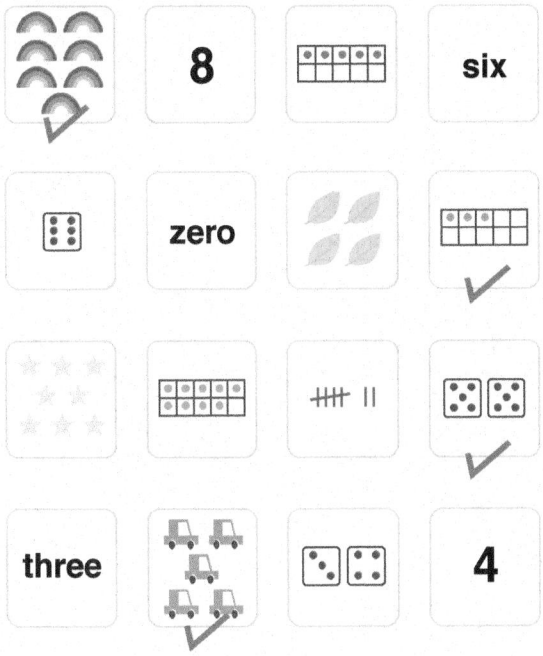

Page 22 • On the Farm

Page 23 • Balloons

Page 24 • Wide Awake

Page 25 • Bouncy Balls

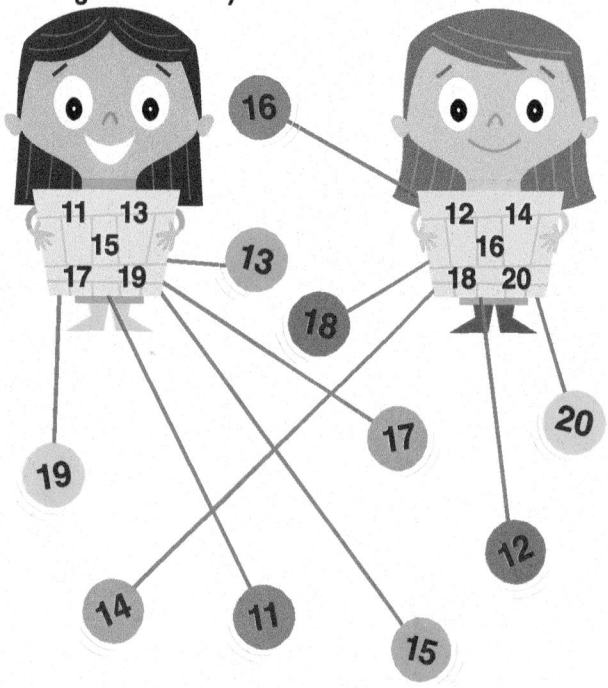

Page 26 • Puzzle Pieces

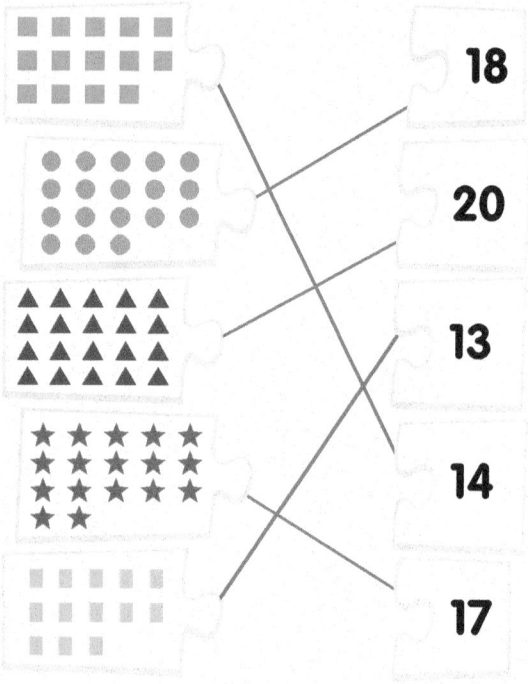

Page 27 • Which Cheetah?

Page 28 • Jack and the Beanstalk

Page 29 • Spider Maze

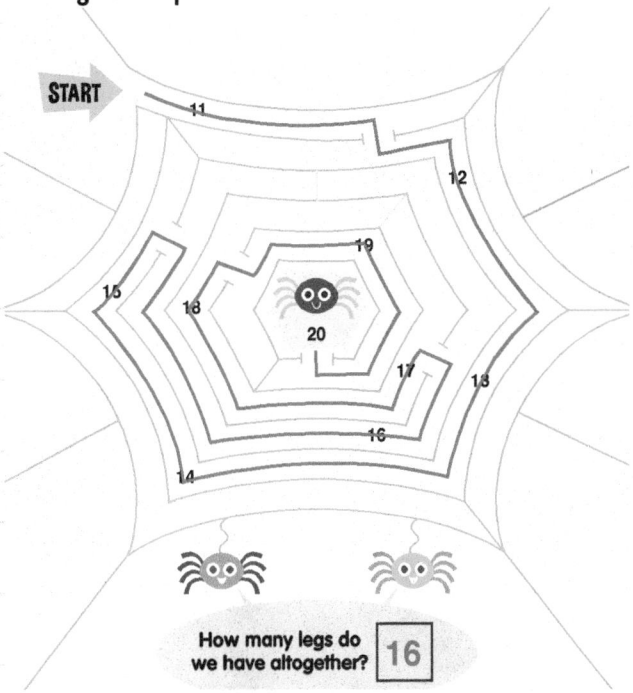

Page 30 • Cupcakes

Page 31 • At the Fairground

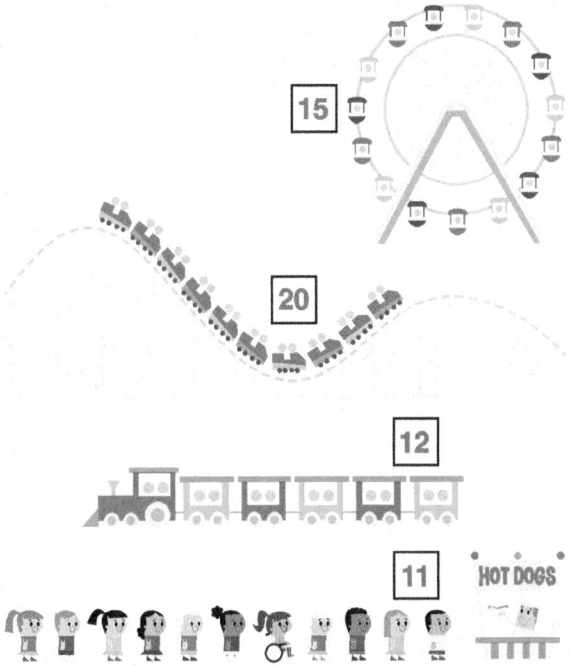

Page 32 • Rainbow Snail

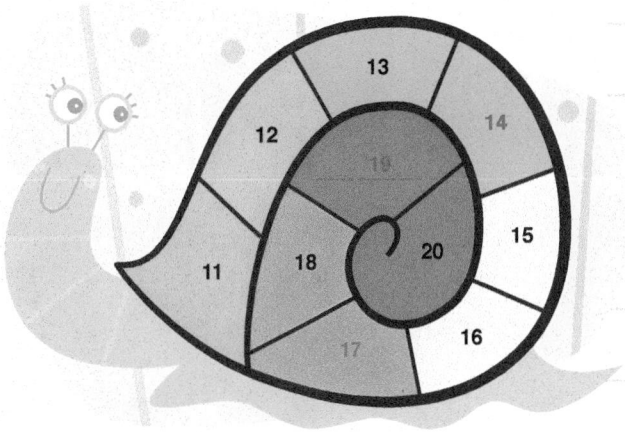

Page 33 • Flowerpots

Page 34 • Number Squares (11–20)

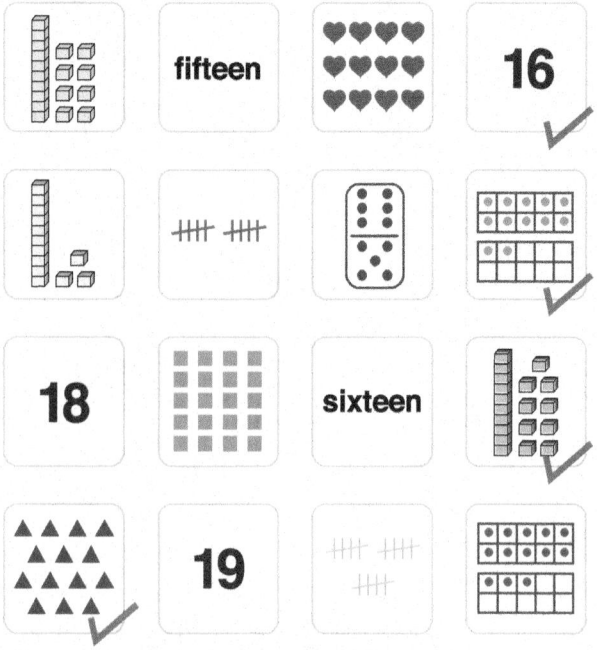

Chapter 3

Page 36 • Sandcastles

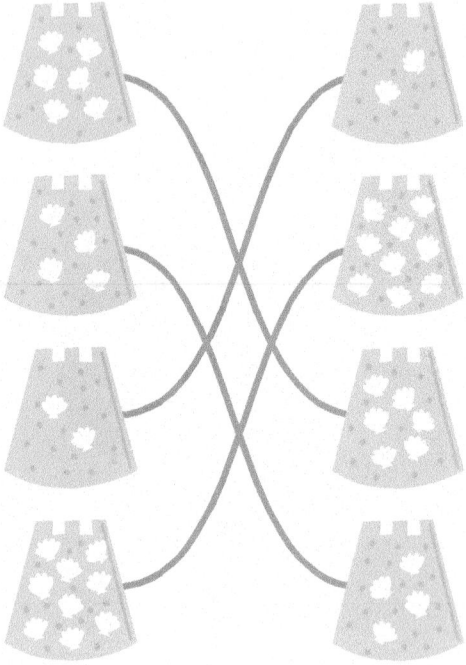

Page 37 • Peapods

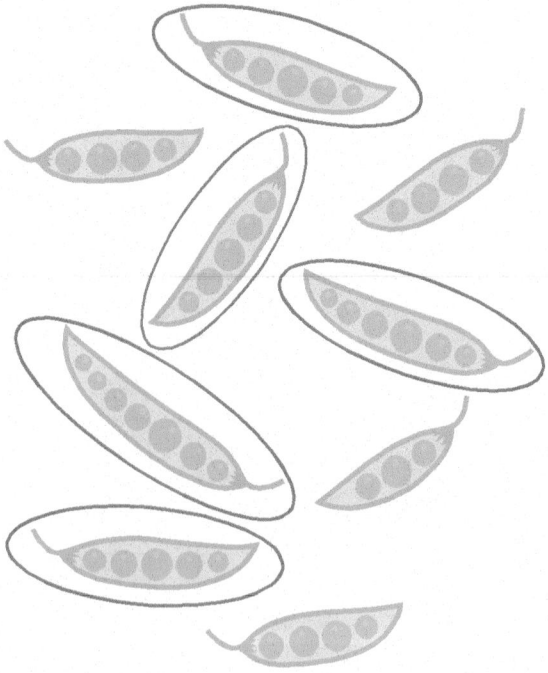

Page 38 • Butterflies

Page 39 • Watermelon Seeds

Page 40 • Which Dog?

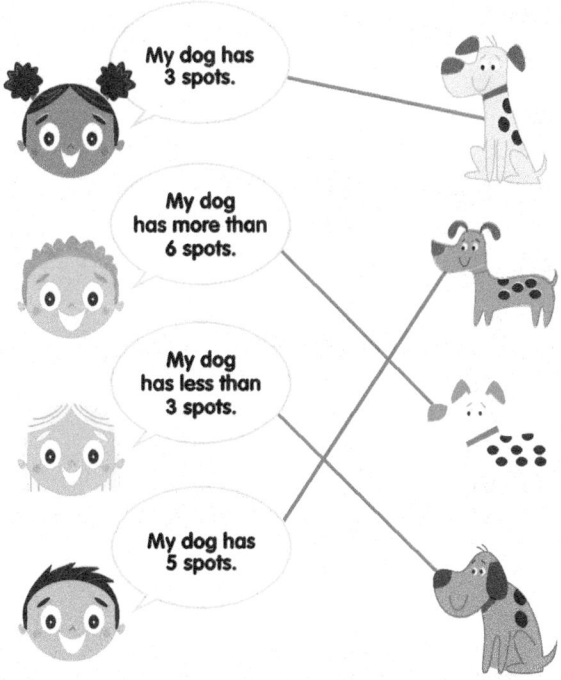

Page 41 • Dinosaurs

Page 42 • Number Pies

1

0

7

5

Page 43 • Crocodiles

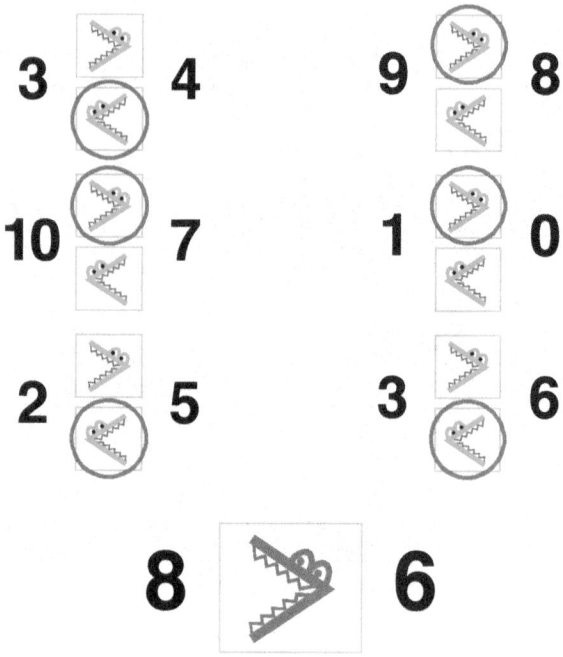

Page 44 • Pizzas

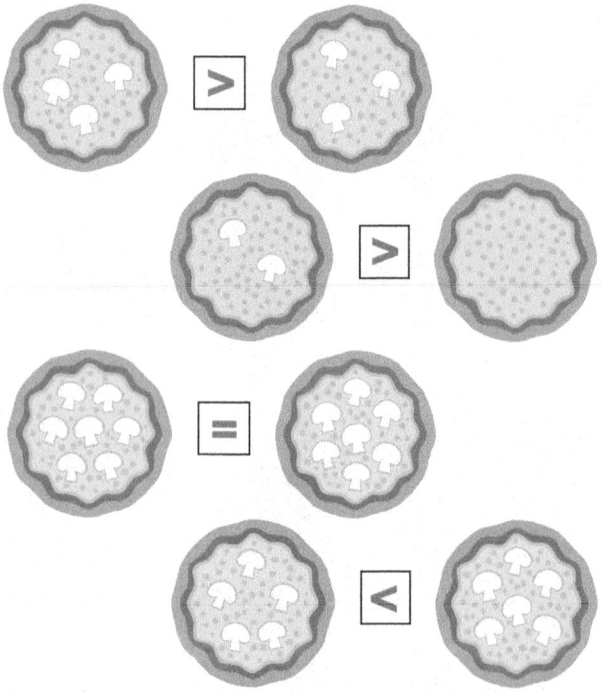

Page 45 • Marbles

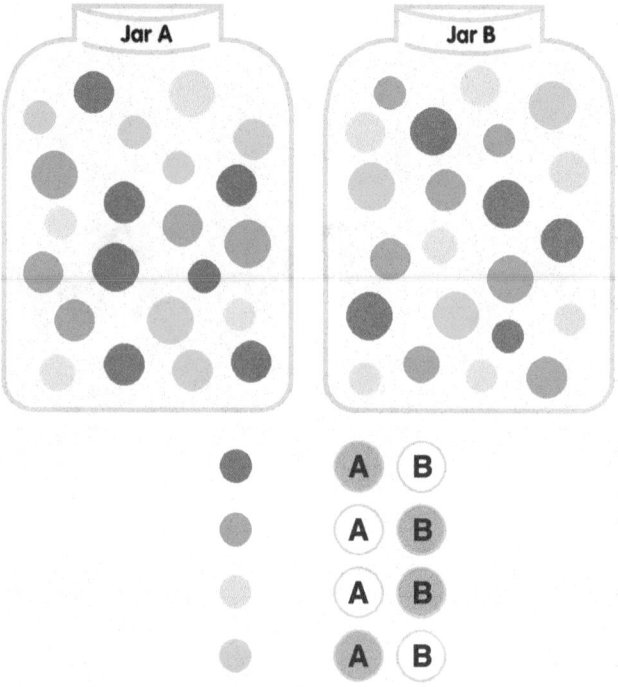

Page 46 • Storming the Castle

Page 47 • Apples

Chapter 4

Page 50 • Houses

23 29 25

20 30

Page 51 • Polly

Page 52 • Trains

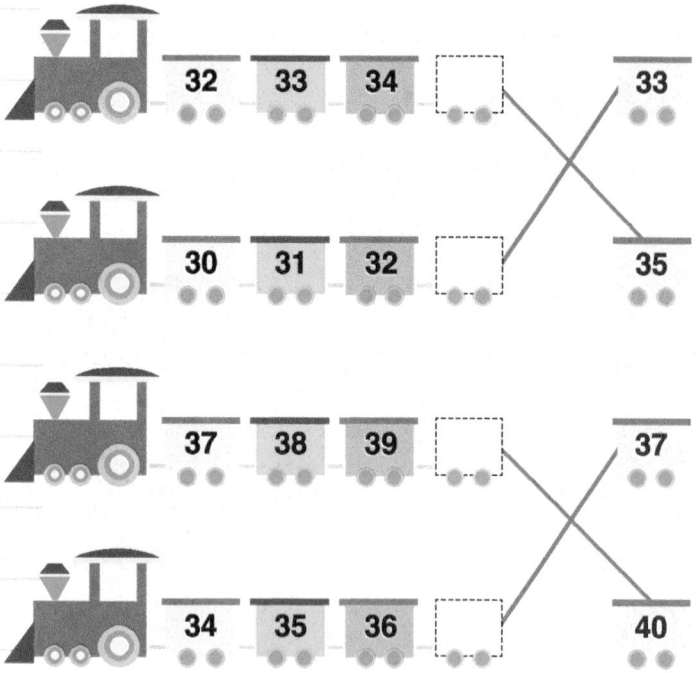

Page 53 • Caterpillars

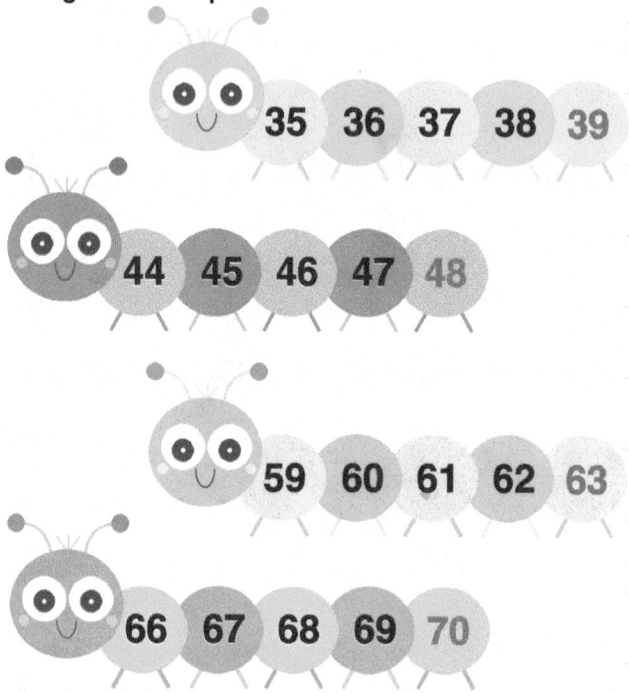

Page 54 • Bird's Nest

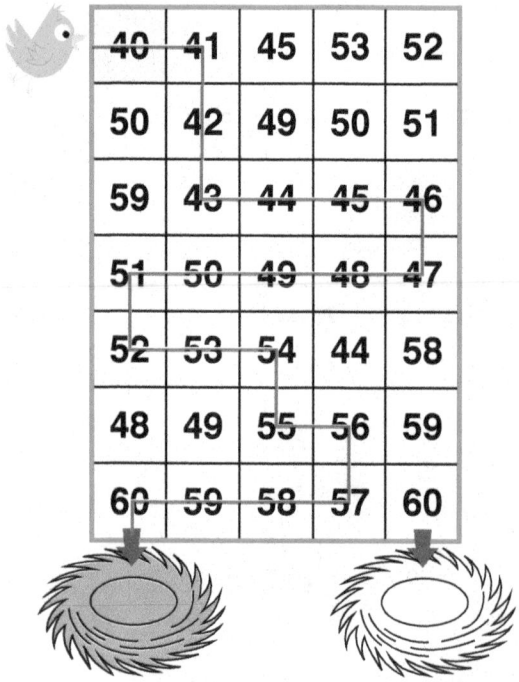

40	41	45	53	52
50	42	49	50	51
59	43	44	45	46
51	50	49	48	47
52	53	54	44	58
48	49	55	56	59
60	59	58	57	60

Page 55 • What's My Name?

1	2	3	4	5	6	7	8	9	10
11	12	13	14	15	16	17	18	19	20
21	22	23	24	25	26	27	28	29	30
31	32	33	34	35	36	37	38	39	40
41	42	43	44	45	46	47	48	49	50
51	52	53	54	55	56	57	58	59	60
61	62	63	64	65	66	67	68	69	70
71	72	73	74	75	76	77	78	79	80
81	82	83	84	85	86	87	88	89	90
91	92	93	94	95	96	97	98	99	100

Page 56 • Up in the Sky

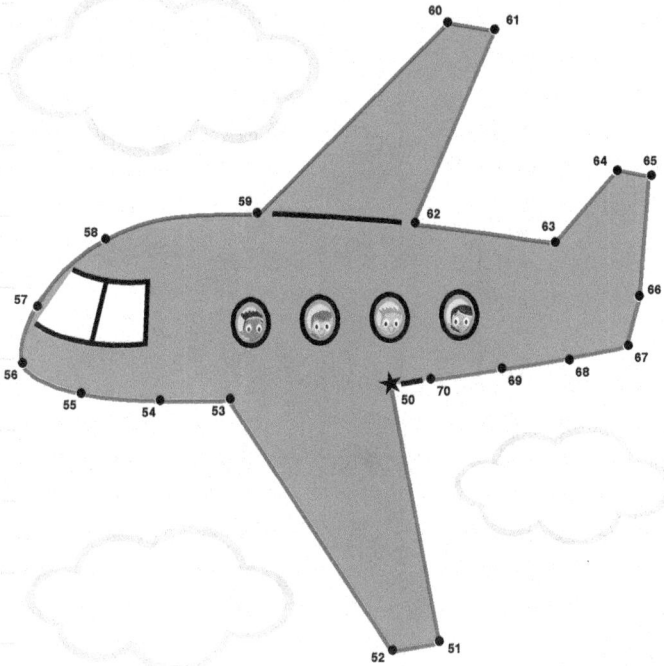

Page 57 • Paint Splatters

1	2	3	4	5	6	7	8	9	10
11	12	13	14	15	16	17	18	19	20
21	22	23	24	25	26	27	28	29	30
31	32	33	34	35	36	37	38	39	40
41	42	43	44	45	46	47	48	49	50
51	52	53	54	55	56	57	58	59	60
61	62	63	64	65	66	67	68	69	70
71	72	73	74	75	76	77	78	79	80
81	82	83	84	85	86	87	88	89	90
91	92	93	94	95	96	97	98	99	100

Page 58 • Who's Swimming?

Page 59 • Counting Crayons

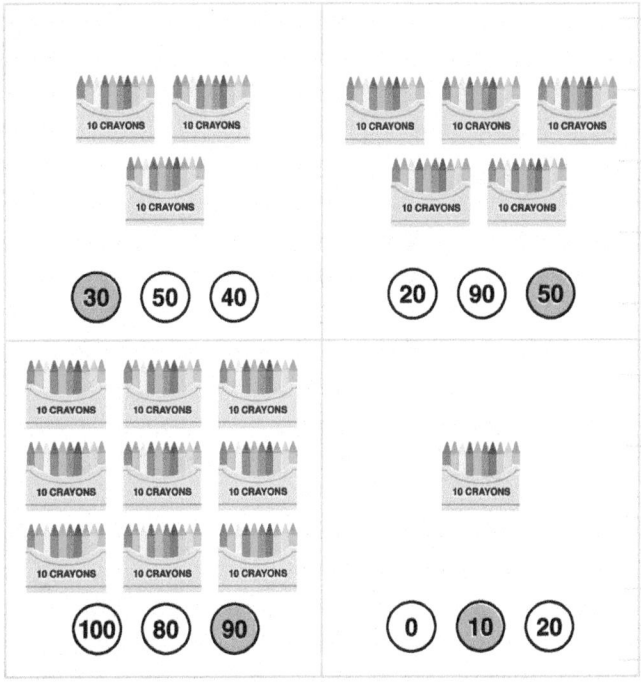

Page 60 • Party Penguins

Page 61 • Jumping Frog

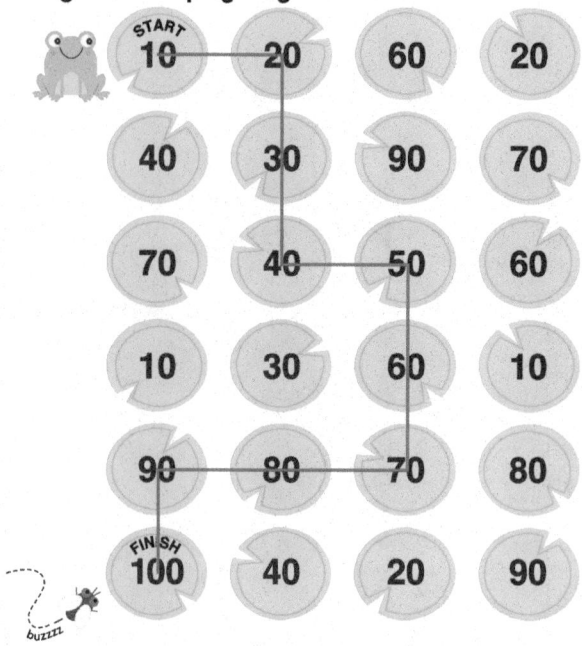

Chapter 5

Page 64 • Ducklings

Page 65 • Which Carrot?

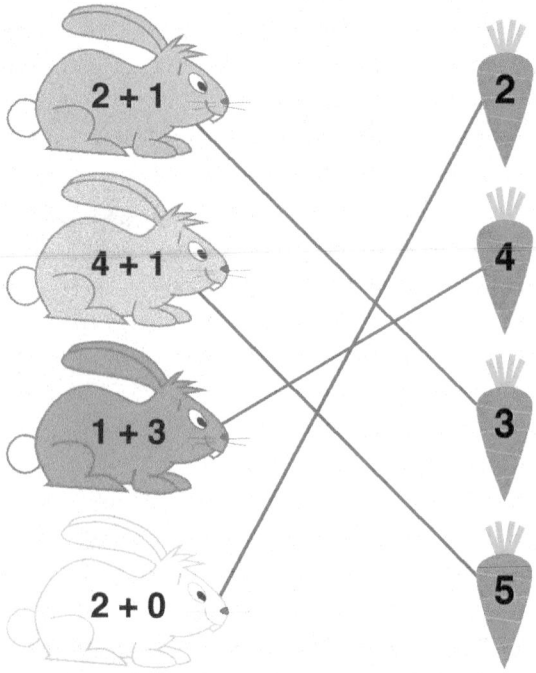

Page 66 • Sunflower

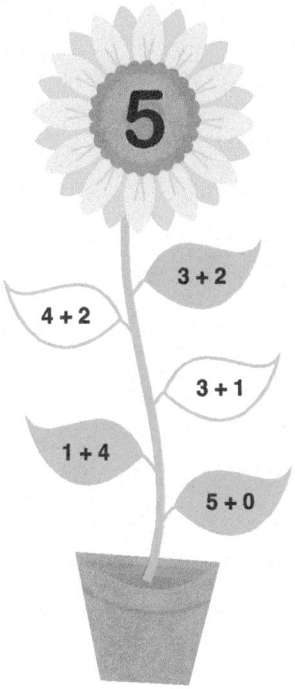

Page 67 • Let's Play!

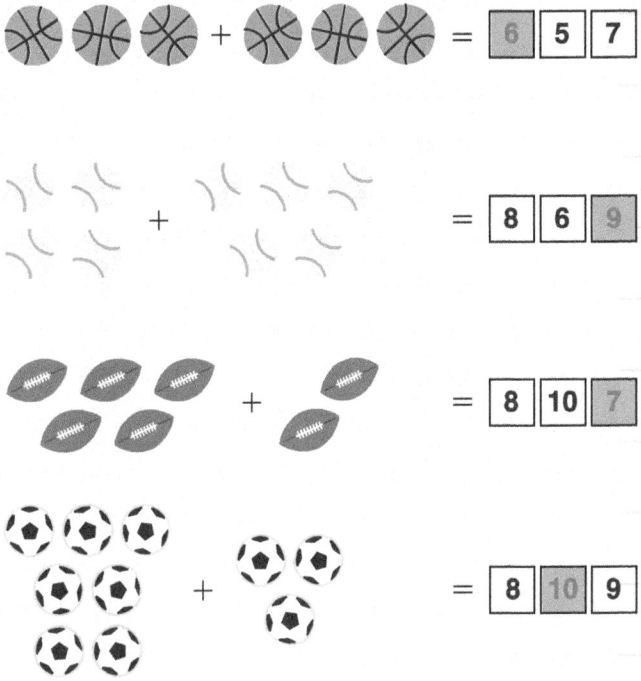

Page 68 • Library Books

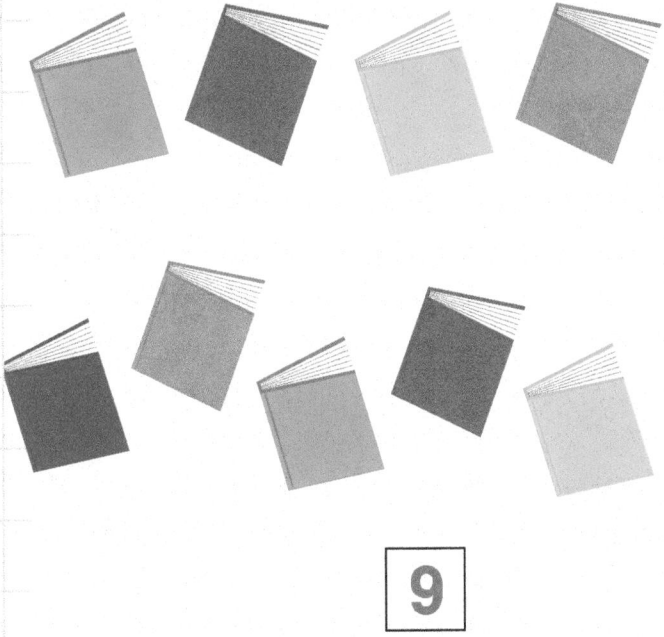

Page 69 • In the Rainforest

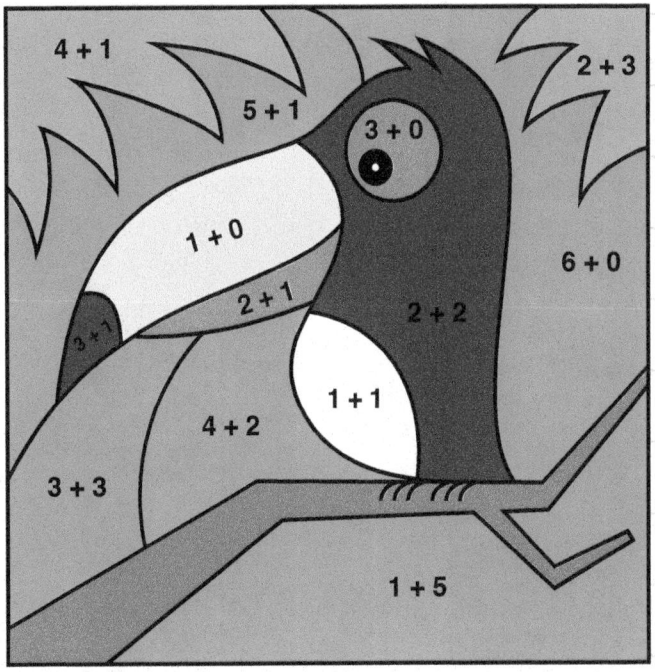

Page 70 • Dice

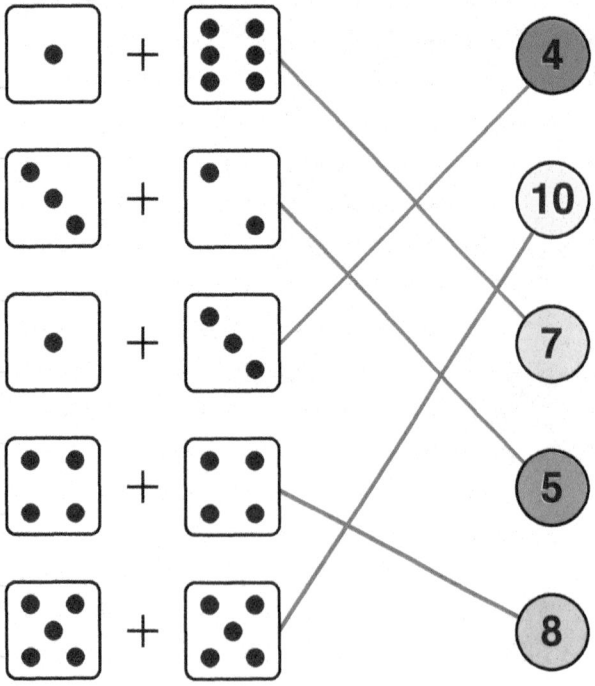

Page 71 • Hamburgers

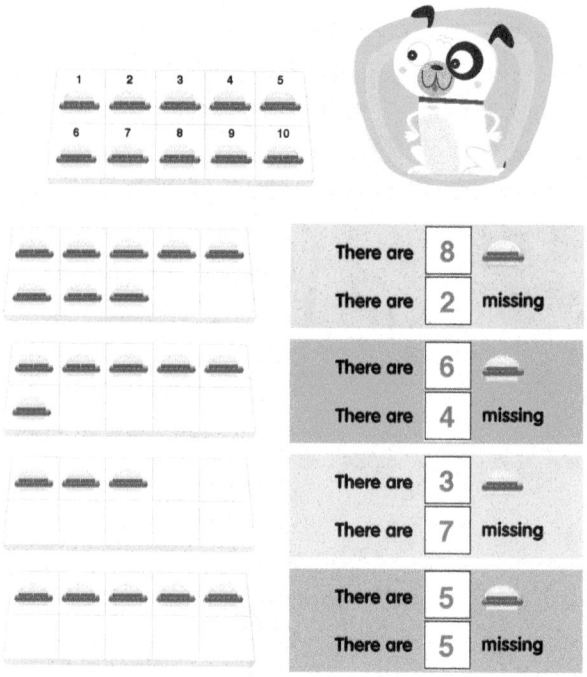

Page 72 • Strawberry Picking

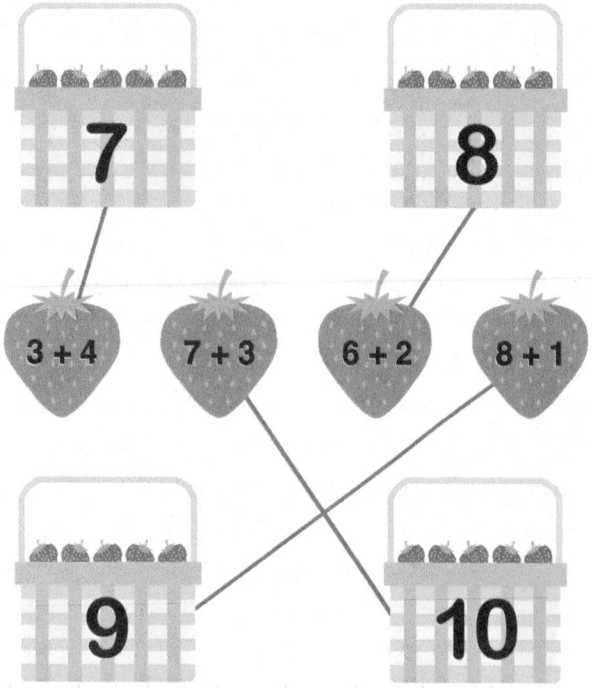

Page 73 • Twins

Chapter 6

Page 74 • Hot-Air Balloons

Page 76 • Fruit Salad

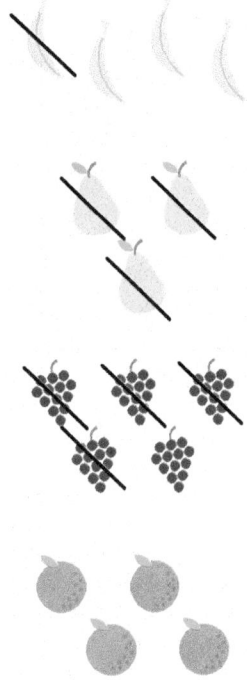

4 – 1 = 3

3 – 3 = 0

5 – 4 = 1

4 – 0 = 4

Page 77 • At the Bakery

Page 78 • Hats

Page 79 • Squirrels

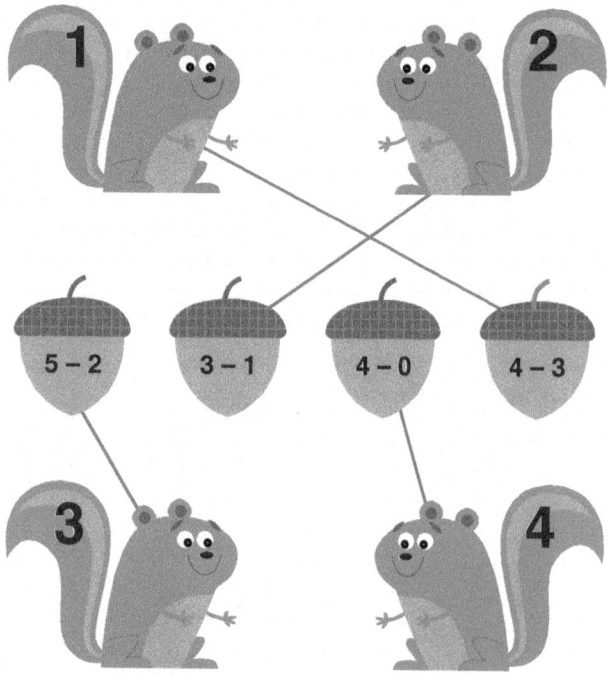

Page 80 • Bears and Honey

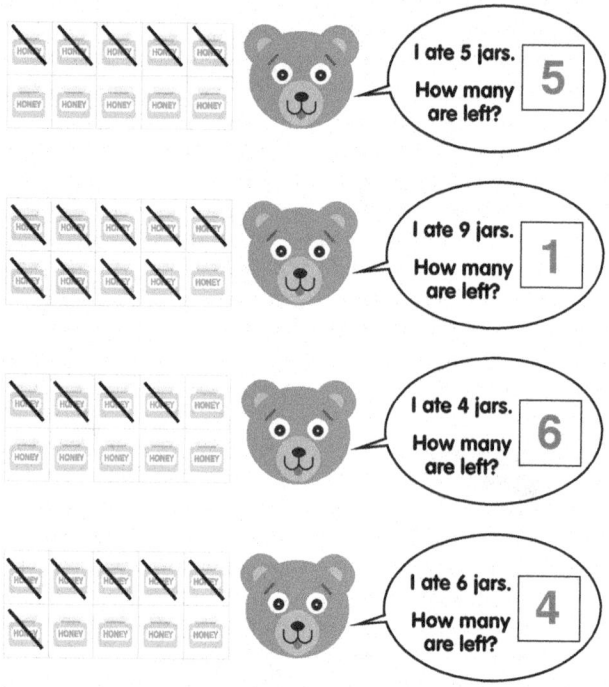

Page 81 • Bees

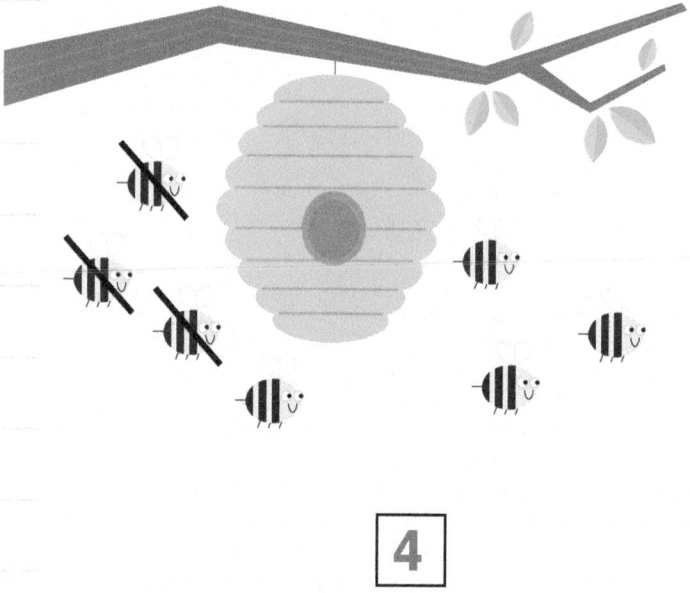

Page 82 • Fishing

Page 83 • On the Beach

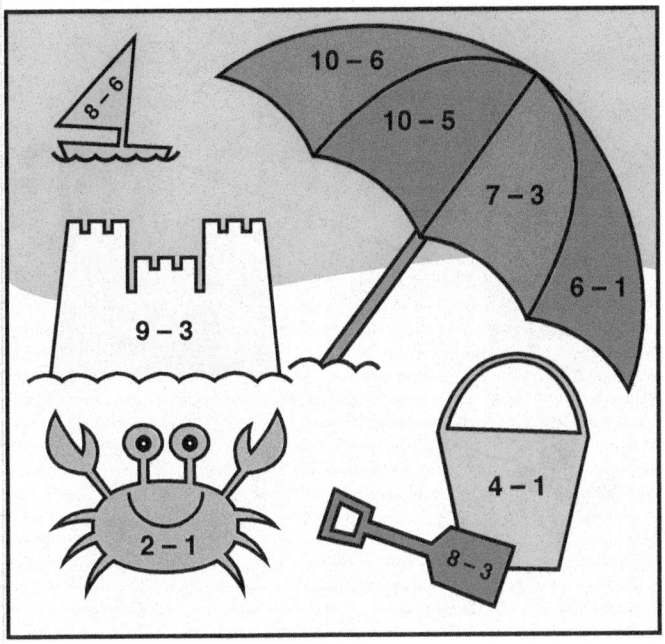

Page 84 • Flying Saucers

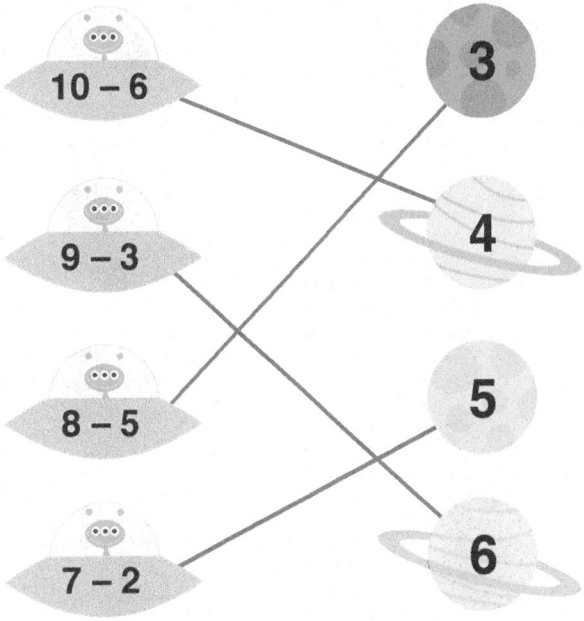

Chapter 7

Page 85 • Happy or Sad?

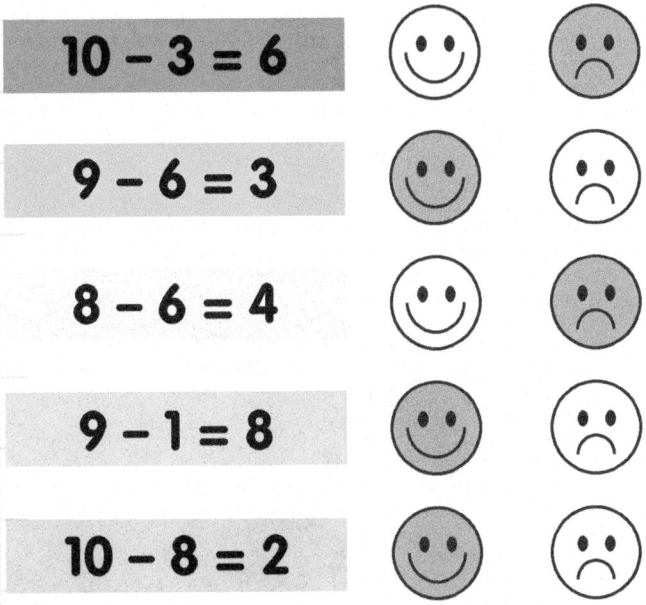

Page 88 • Which Animal?

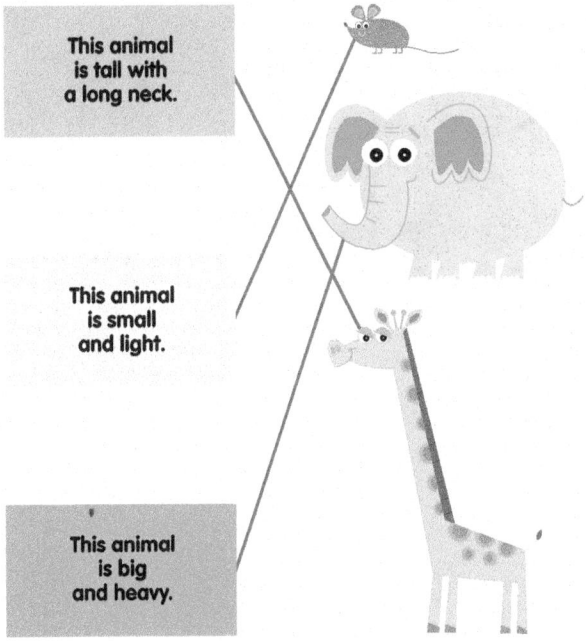

Page 89 • Sorting Socks

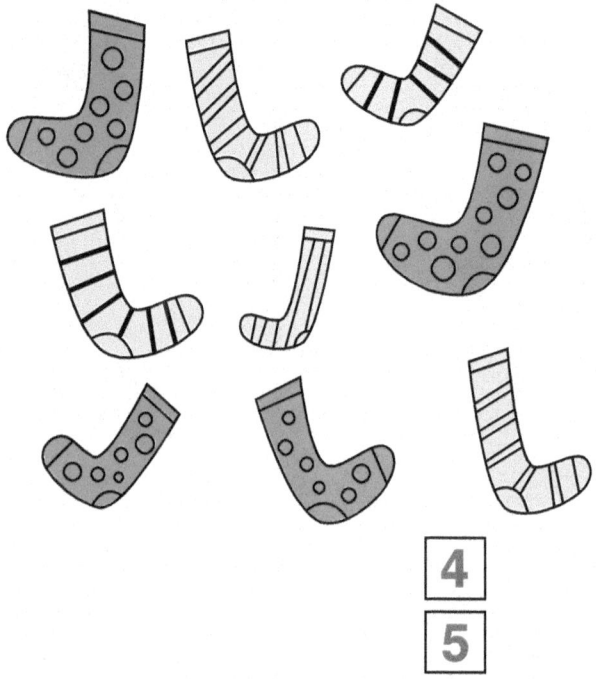

Page 90 • Legs

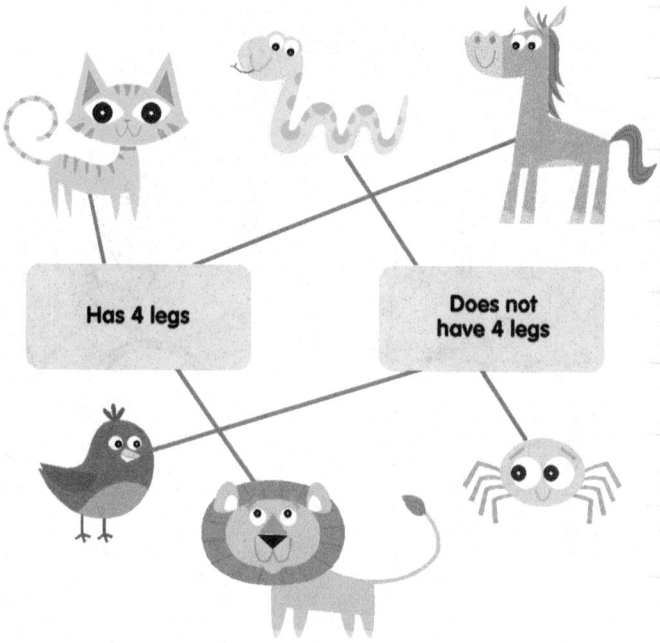

Page 91 • Snowmen

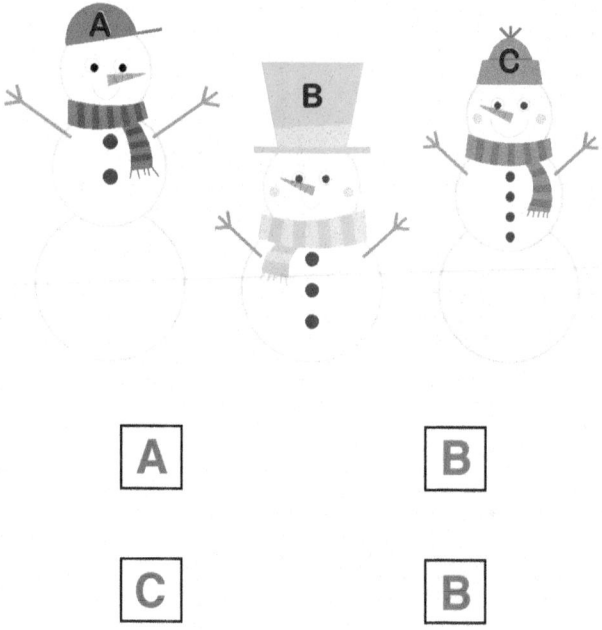

Page 92 • In the Backyard

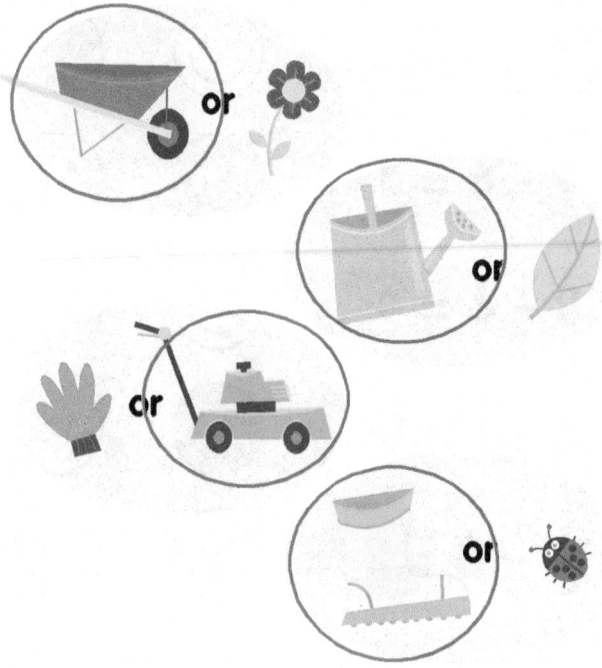

Page 93 • Pairs

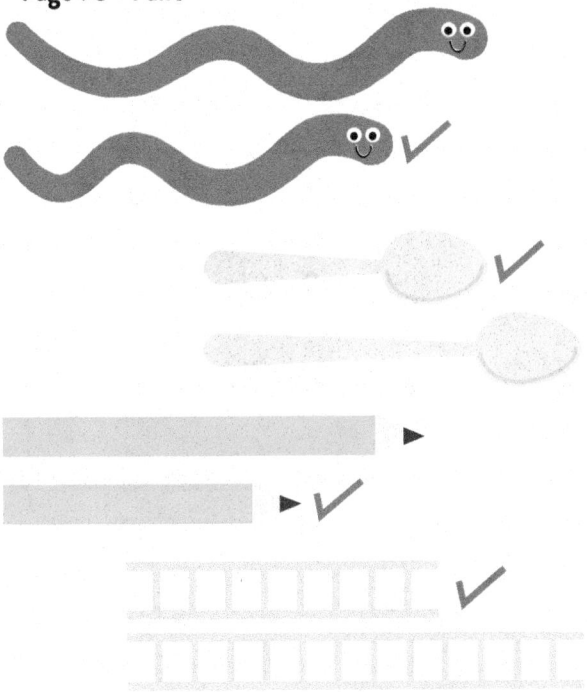

Page 94 • Gifts

Page 95 • On the Move

Page 96 • Pencil Case

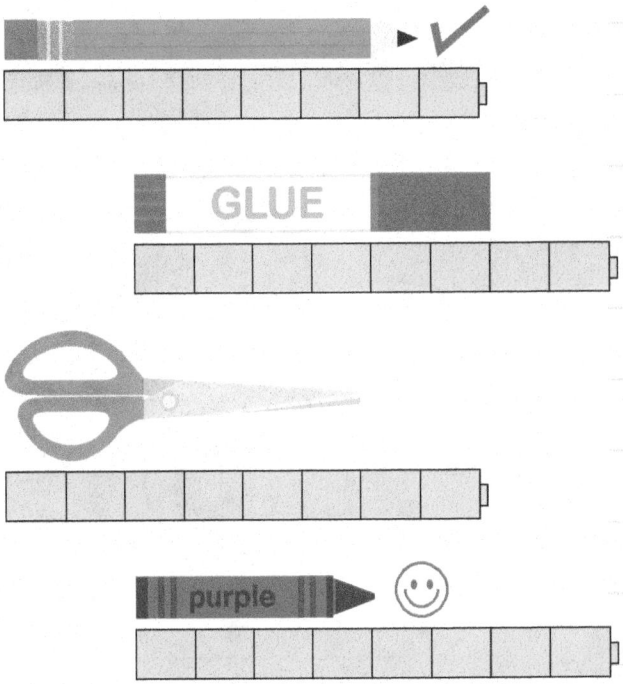

Page 97 • Enchanted Forest

Page 98 • Water

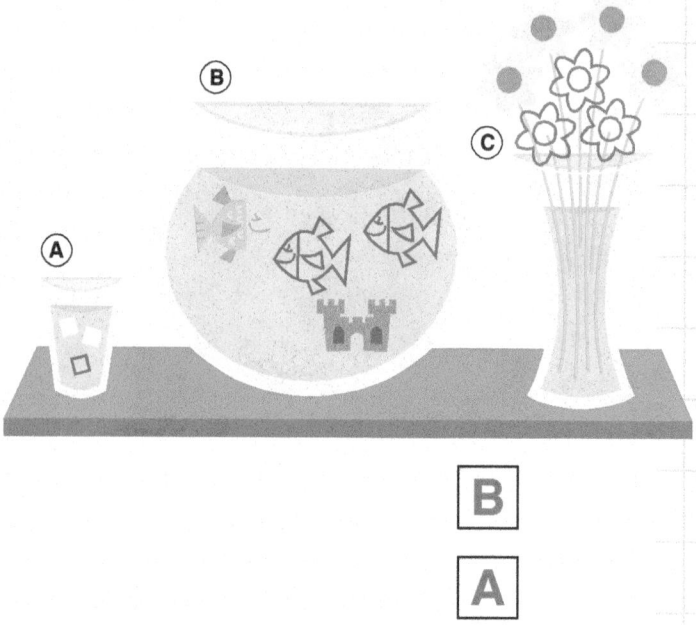

Page 99 • How's the Weather?

Page 100 • Jelly Beans

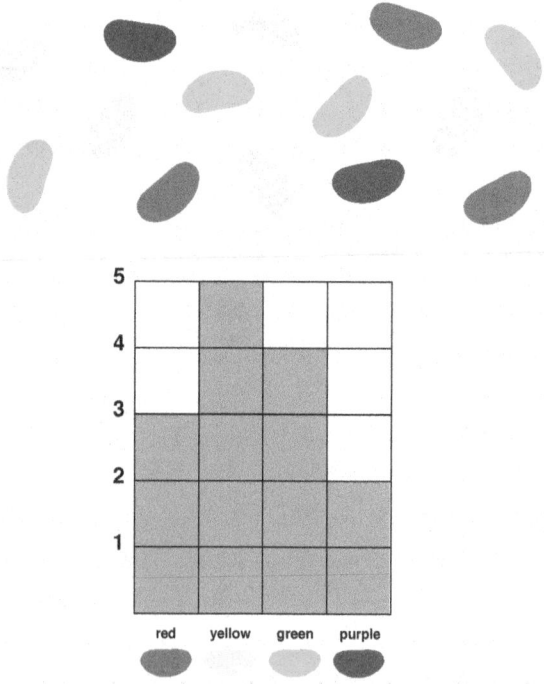

Chapter 8

Page 102 • Everyday Shapes

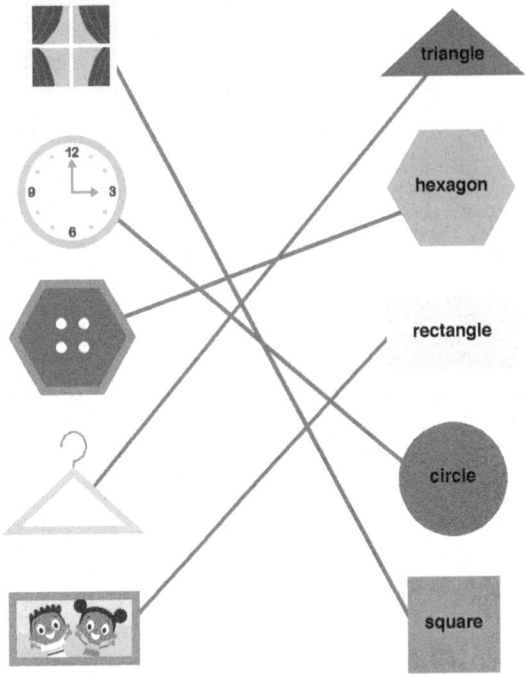

Page 103 • Mice and Cheese

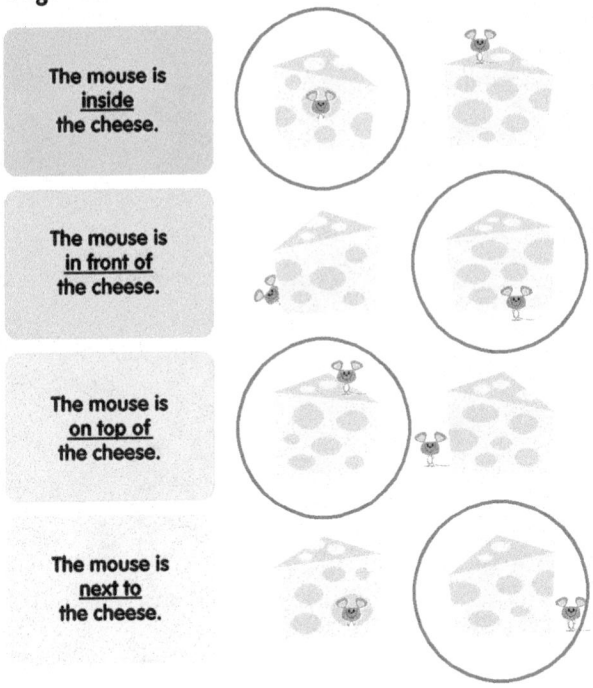

Page 104 • Jewels

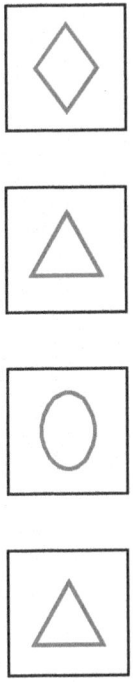

Page 105 • Design a Hat

Page 106 • Kites

Page 107 • Robot

Page 108 • Cookies

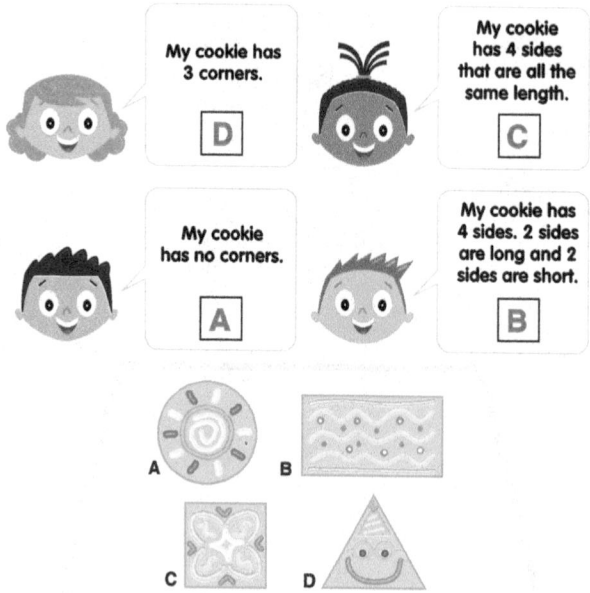

Page 109 • Shape Pictures

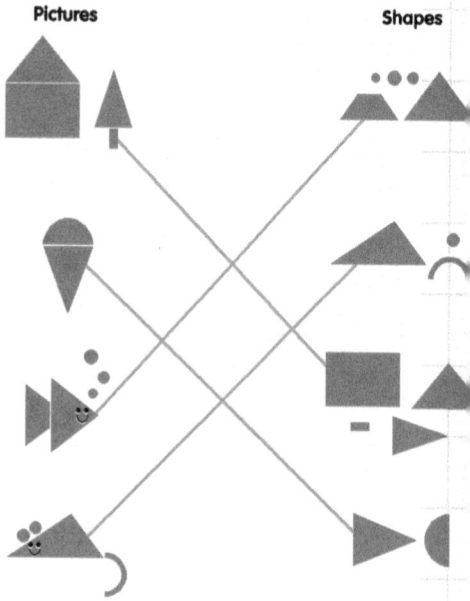

Page 110 • Flat or Solid?

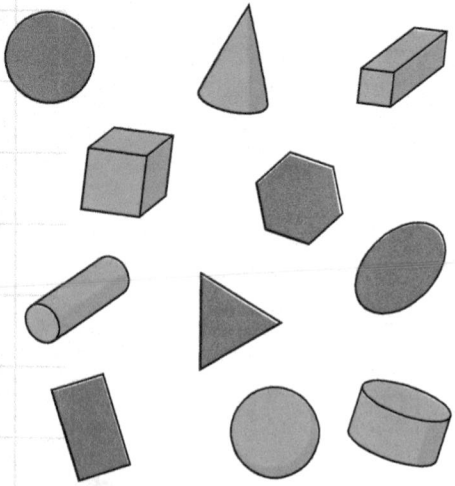

Page 111 • Shape People

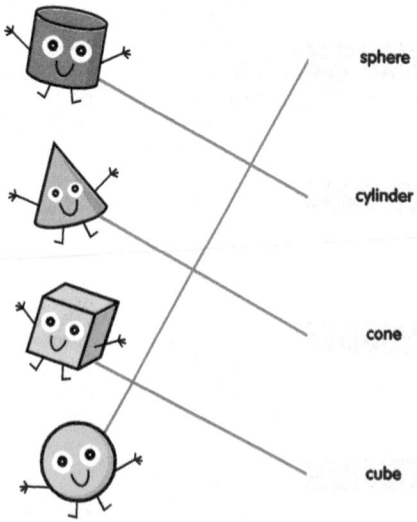

Page 112 • Traffic Light

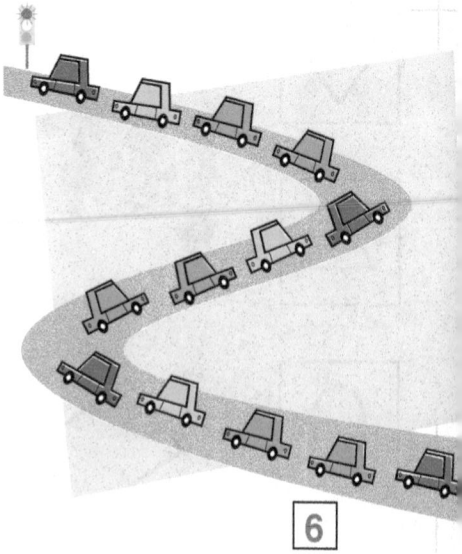

Page 113 • Shapes All Around

Page 114 • Toy Store

The  is **in front of** / **beside** the 

The  is **above** / **below** the 

The  is **behind** / **beside** the 

The  is **below** / **above** the 

Page 115 • What Am I?

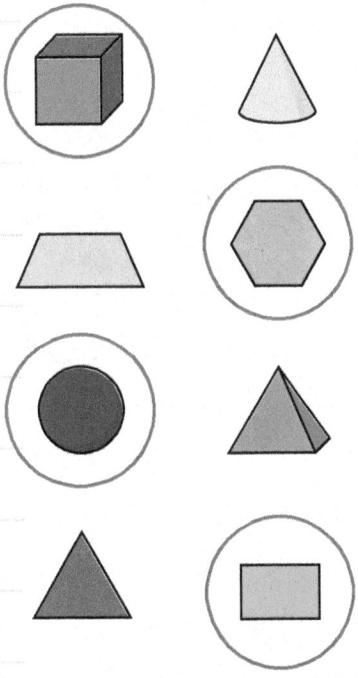

Page 116 • Cone or Cylinder?

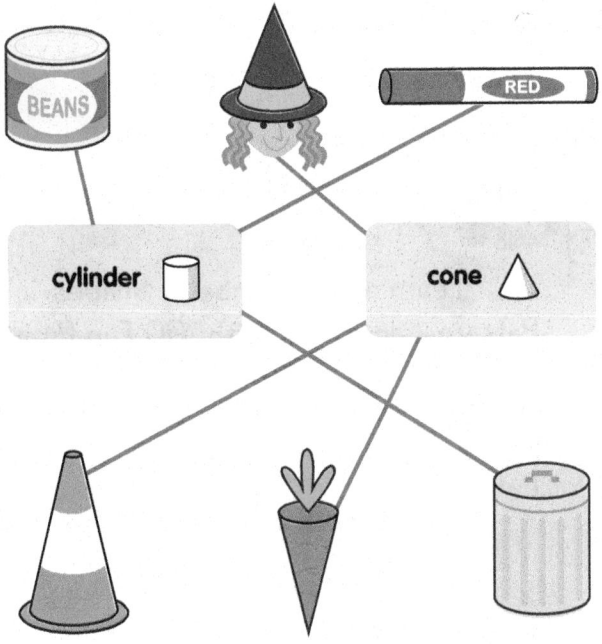

Page 117 • What Is Missing?

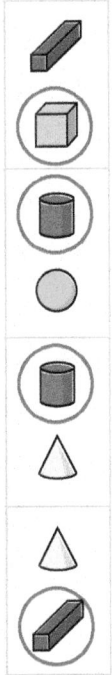

MATH PUZZLES AND ACTIVITIES

your pre-K student is sure to love!

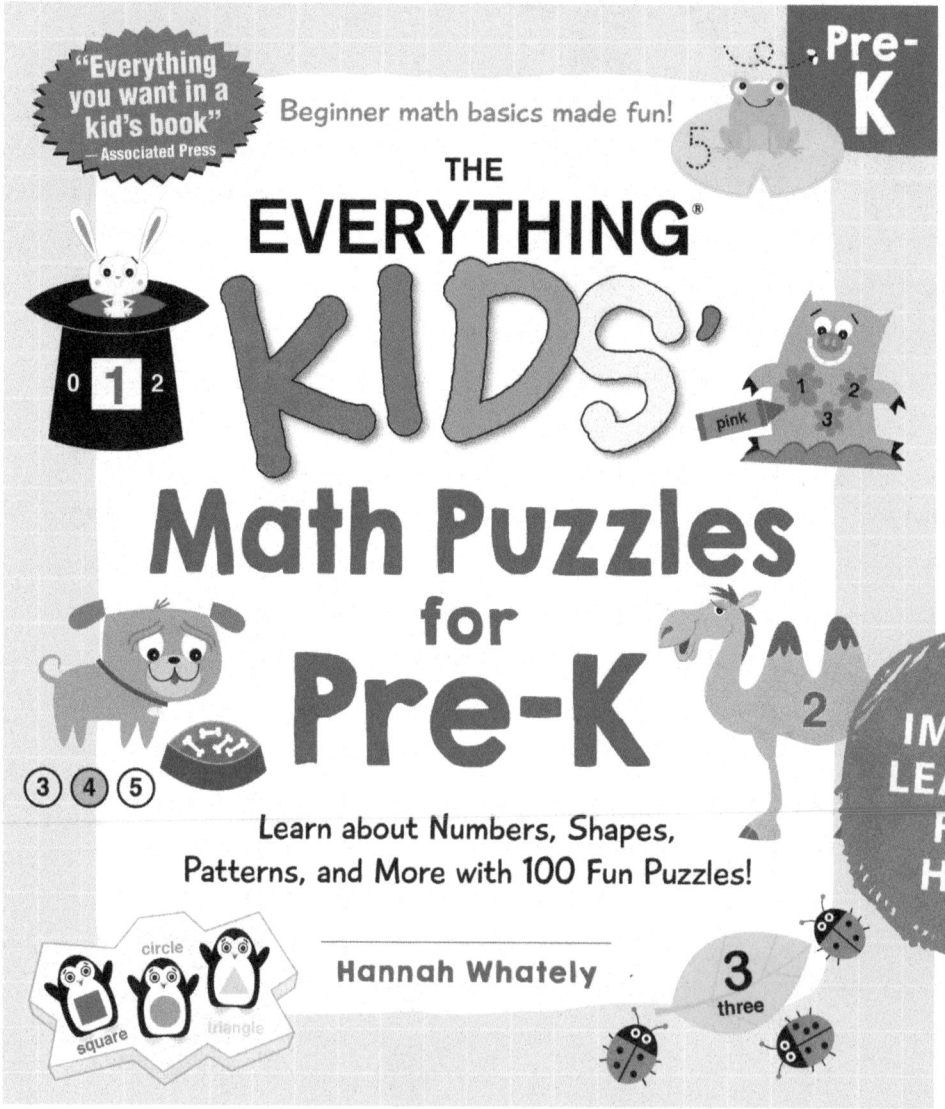

PICK UP OR DOWNLOAD YOUR COPY TODAY!

adamsmedia
An Imprint of Simon & Schuster
A ViacomCBS COMPANY